The Voice
of the Folk

The Voice of the Folk

Folklore and American Literary Theory

GENE BLUESTEIN

University of Massachusetts Press

For Ellie
and to the memory of
Irvin Jay Weir
Born January 29, 1909
Grove, Oklahoma
Died January 29, 1968
Riverside, California

For a second let me turn aside
and say that the beginning of
literary form is in some turn
given to the sentence in folk speech.
Art is the amplification and
sophistication of the proverbial
turns of speech.

ROBERT FROST

Acknowledgments

I OWE a great debt to my teachers at Brooklyn College and the University of Minnesota, especially: Frederic Ewen, Thelma Lavine, Harry Slochower, Leo Marx, Samuel Holt Monk, and Henry Nash Smith. Professor Smith read the manuscript and attempted to hold me to the high standards he has always set for his students. My colleagues at Fresno State College, Roger Chittick and Peter Everwine, gave me the benefit of their good advice. Philip Levine directed me to some sources I would otherwise have missed.

Joseph J. Kwiat directed my first attempt to deal with American folk tradition. His humane response to my efforts has provided a model for my own relations with students, and his advice has served me equally well in the present study. I trust that none of the foregoing will be held guilty by association with what I have done to their best contributions to the community of scholarship.

Two Carnegie Foundation Fellowships in American Studies awarded by the University of Minnesota gave me the opportunity to study American folksongs in the field. The book was completed under a Research Leave granted by the California State Colleges.

My approach to folk music has been shaped largely by the work of Charles Seeger and his son, Pete Seeger. No one who has been interested in folk music should neglect to thank Moses Asch, whose *Folkways Catalogue* is evidence of his great achievement.

Much of what is discussed here at length was published, in a variety of forms and in briefer compass, in the *Journal of the History of Ideas, The New England Quarterly, Southern Folklore Quarterly, The Texas Quarterly,* and *Western Folklore.* "The Blues as a Literary Theme" and "The Poetry of Rock" were first published in *The Massachusetts Review.* The latter was originally presented as a paper at a meeting of the Annual Modern Literature Conference sponsored by Michigan State University in 1969.

The epigraph is taken from *Interviews with Robert Frost,* Edwin Connery Latham, ed. (New York: Holt, Rinehart & Winston, 1966), p. 7, with permission.

The dedication to my wife is in gratitude for her contributions as typist, editor, critic, and friend. Irv Weir would have enjoyed more than anyone seeing this in print—especially if it stirs up some controversy.

I'm pleased to record my thanks to Paul Wright of the University of Massachusetts Press, whose editorial suggestions I found, on the whole, irresistible.

Fresno, California, 1971

Contents

Introduction

THIS STUDY is concerned mainly with the relationships between folklore and American literary theory; such relationships obviously exist, but their significance in American literary history has been largely overlooked. Assumptions about the connections between folklore and literature appear generally in the realm of ideology—that is, they represent theoretical constructs which seem to be justifications of rather widely held points of view. When followed to their source, they almost always lead to the views of the German philosopher, historian, and folklorist, Johann Gottfried von Herder (1744–1803). Since the eighteenth century Herder has been associated with folk ideology, but with the exception of the small number of scholars who have studied his work closely his ideas have been related to the traditions of extreme nationalism and racism which flourished in Europe during the nineteenth century. The germ of my interest in Herder came from the discovery that both Emerson and Whitman had found his conceptions congenial to their programs for the development of an indigenous literature in the United States. But although the lines of contact between the Emerson-Whitman tradition and Herder are clear, I have not been concerned basically to trace sources. My fundamental interest is to expose the origin of some central ideas in American culture, and it has been valuable to discover that many have deep roots in the civilization of the Old World.

Consequently, while the ideas of Herder form a discernible thread through the fabric of issues dealt with here, it is also important to note the peculiar variations in the design as it appeared in this country. A notable instance is the work of Constance Rourke, in which there is a conscious application of Herderian ideas to the conditions of the American experience. Miss Rourke's contribution to the field of American Studies has been widely acknowledged but in a generally offhand manner. I have attempted not only to pay close attention to her insights into the relationships between folklore and American literature, but also to note elements in her work which are related to the Emerson-Whitman tradition.

At the same time I have emphasized the close affinities between Miss Rourke's pioneering efforts to establish the sources of an American folklore tradition and the equally significant work of John and Alan

Lomax. The latter have been accorded a fate similar to Miss Rourke's; no one will deny the impressive accomplishments of the Lomaxes in providing evidence of a rich and variegated tradition of American folksong. But academic folklorists have sometimes too cavalierly dismissed the ideological implications of their work, which are argued closely along the lines that I discuss in the early chapters of this study.

Although the Lomaxes insisted on the germinal force of Negro folklore and folksong, little attention has been paid to the ideological implications of black tradition in American literature. I have examined several attempts to use black sources in formal fiction, especially in the work of William Faulkner and Ralph Ellison. The use of these materials provides us with a contemporary example of a strategy employed by writers since Emerson and Whitman to define the meaning of American literary tradition and relate it to the crucial issues raised by our development.

Finally, I have made some comments on the "rock scene." Although it may be too early to make major predictions about its future, the phenomenon of rock music and lyrics constitutes a development from the traditions I have discussed here and indicates the persistence of ideological and esthetic approaches worked out up until this time within the context of folklore and formal literature. What I have discerned in the rock tradition is a similar movement within the context of popular culture. (A related phenomenon which I cannot discuss in this study is the use in post-World-War-II fiction of materials derived from jazz; in *Invisible Man*, Ellison focuses on Louis Armstrong to define a folk-jazz ideology. But so much has occurred in jazz since Armstrong that a special study is warranted.)

What binds these figures together—the European philosopher, the American writers, critics, and folklorists—is the belief that the highest cultural values can be derived from what cultivated classes often describe condescendingly as the vulgar, lowest levels of society. During the eighteenth century in Germany it seemed unlikely for such a view to be expressed, yet Herder developed it fully. In nineteenth-century America (under the influence of what was to become in George Santayana's phrase the Genteel Tradition) it seemed equally difficult to entertain such a notion; but Emerson and Whitman voiced the belief that it was so. And in our time Constance Rourke and the Lomaxes continued to argue the same propositions, despite the objections of genteel critics. A similar argument is being made today by black writers in behalf of a current of culture consistently excluded from the mainstream of American life.

The underlying commitment of all these figures and groups, however, is more than mere ideology. It was based on the most sophisticated insights into the nature of language, literature, social structure, and political philosophy; and in a contemporary context, the traditions under discussion here continue to illuminate the meaning of American art and life. All the writers who interest me in this study attempt to deal with the problems raised by the traditional opposition between folk and formal art, the first conceived to be "child-like," primitive, and unaware of its techniques; the second defined as mature, civilized, and conscious of its craftsmanship. Here is the point of connection with American literary theory, for in citing the deficiencies of folk art, we have also recalled the continuing critique of American literature as immature and flawed by the formal lapses of its creators. The causes of these limitations are conceived to be many, but a persistent idea is that they are inevitable consequences of the American experience, which has apparently led many of our writers to reject both the ideological and the technical accomplishments of their European antecedents. The American writer is by birth and inclination *peau rouge*, "the great Western Barbarian," as Henry James allowed Mrs. Tristram to characterize Christopher Newman in *The American*. To Newman's response that he is not literally an Indian, Mrs. Tristram concedes: "I don't mean that you are a Comanche chief, or that you wear a blanket and feathers. There are different shades." And as James might have said, "There it is." Sooner or later, and despite his civilized disguise, the American will reveal his true colors.

Like most American writers, James expended a good deal of energy to prove that his protagonists were truly civilized and sensitive despite their cultural limitations. But James's strategy took those limitations almost at face value. His Americans have a certain honesty and vitality, but they need to be tempered by exposure to the advantages (and especially the discipline) of high culture. The Indian (the Negro will do as well) may be fascinatingly exotic, but no one can take his poetry or music seriously.

The approach that interests me in this study takes another tack. It argues in general that the lower layers of society are not at all devoid of cultural significance. In fact they are conceived to be the major source of materials which sophisticated society uses to fashion its literary expression; and these original materials are acknowledged to be esthetically valid in their own terms. (Precisely how folk materials can be used in formal literature is a question that has posed major problems and I will argue that Emerson provided a viable solution.) At the same time the writers I am concerned with emphasize the historical appropriateness for the United States to make explicit its reliance on "vulgar" traditions as a source of its literary accomplishments.

I would add one caveat: the tradition I have tried to define here will not explain all of American literary development, nor is it meant to. Despite the fact that its assumptions sometimes show up in unlikely places (in elements of T. S. Eliot's esthetic, for example), other writers (like James) have found little of value for them in the esthetic that emanates from Emerson and Whitman. Nevertheless, the Emerson-Whitman tradition as I have defined it represents a major development in American literary history and deserves, as I attempt to show in the pages that follow, the close attention that I have given it.

Chapter One
Folklore and Ideology

SINCE THE eighteenth century every discussion of folklore and folk-song has presupposed an integral relationship between national literary traditions and the body of folk art produced by unsophisticated or even illiterate people. The nature of that relationship, as we shall see, is susceptible of a variety of interpretations, but there has rarely been any question that it exists. Indeed even if we go back to the very be-ginnings of literary criticism in Western tradition we find the same idea operating. It was, for example, one of the bases for Aristotle's approach in his estimate of the development of Greek literature. The sources of epic, drama, and lyric poetry he assumed to be the anterior tradition of folklore, myth, and the rituals associated with them, and it seemed logical to discuss the highest accomplishments of conscious literary endeavors in terms of the folk (and essentially oral) traditions that preceded them. The Homeric poems raised the issue even more clearly, for here was a body of materials that were themselves folk and oral in nature. Aristotle knew very well (as a good many modern readers still do not) that the *Odyssey* and the *Iliad* were originally folksongs, performed by minstrels whose main function was to pre-serve the heritage of oral tradition. Often with musical accompaniment, the stories associated with heroes and gods were presented to large and varied audiences.[1] At a later time when the various sections had been codified it might take several evenings to hear the whole saga of Odysseus or Achilles, but as several scenes in the *Odyssey* reveal, the Greeks were quite willing to put off their games and battles for the pleasure of being entertained and instructed by the bard. A similar reaction seems to control the response of popular audiences in our own time. Even the most casual listener is frequently awed into re-spectful attention by the sense that the folksinger is more than a mere performer, that he is a "representative man," and that the song pro-vides an insight into "the spirit of the people." And despite the fact that folksongs in our time have often become the property of com-mercial music houses, the main attraction of countless night clubs, and the stock in trade of disc-jockeys, the impression still persists that folk-songs somehow transcend the experience of the individual singer and represent the deeper values and emotions of the folk.

By the nineteenth century, the view that a nation's poetry is truly national only to the extent that it is based on the raw material of the country's folklore and song became a fully developed ideological position, with significant implications for the study of history and sociology as well as literature and folklore. For Europeans the terms of this relationship between folklore and literature were relatively easy to define. Folk generally meant peasant, and it could be easily assumed that the creations of this sector of society were quaint, picturesque, and valuable essentially as an expression of "folk wisdom" which the more educated members of society might appreciate despite its acknowledged crudities. But at the same time, there was associated with folk culture a mystique which might be expressed in such terms as national or racial essences that somehow managed to make themselves felt.

In the United States, there were other complicating factors which resulted in substantially different developments from precisely the same issues and attitudes. The basic components were exactly the same. Our writers, especially in the nineteenth century, were concerned to establish some relationship between folk and formally organized literary traditions for the purpose of defining the essential national character of this country. The circumstance provides us with an excellent opportunity to analyze the way in which American thinkers have responded to the heritage of European ideas, reshaping and developing them to serve the needs of their own experience.

The best way to accomplish this is to look closely at the formulations of Johann Gottfried von Herder who provided the fullest statement of a folk ideology which had direct and continuing influence on the approaches of several generations of American writers and scholars. Herder's work has been dealt with in the context of several disciplines. He has been a significant figure in philosophy, history, and sociology, as well as folklore. In the latter field his reputation has been muddled by the attribution to him of attitudes not central to his own approach but which through a kind of guilt by association ally him with extreme nationalist or racist doctrines. The latter have been especially damning, but I think it can be shown that neither in his own writing nor in his influence on those who read him carefully was this the case.

Herder was one of those remarkable figures whose interests led him to activity in several fields. He is acknowledged as one of the founders (along with Giambattista Vico) of the philosophy of history. His speculations about the nature of the national state have made him a crucial figure in political science as well as sociological research.

His investigation of the origins of language was one of several major influences on later linguistic explorations. And his interest in folklore and folksong provide a major statement of a relationship that is still of great concern to writers here and abroad. In some ways, Herder's formulations all hang together and flow one from the other. He was philosophically an organicist who consciously intended to revise the Newtonian and Lockean mechanistic thesis which underlay much of the thinking in his time. While some of these areas of his interest will be relevant to my own argument, I will be concerned essentially with his approach to the relationships between folklore and formal literature and their significance in the development of our national literary tradition.

Herder's interest in folksong was precipitated by his reading of Bishop Thomas Percy's *Reliques of Ancient English Poetry,* which was published in 1765. Although it was not the first investigation of English folksong tradition, Albert B. Friedman points out that "it summarizes and climaxes the neoclassic interest in the ballads; and since it largely determined the lines which the appreciation of popular poetry took thereafter, it is the most influential book in the romantic phase of the revival as well."[2] Despite the criticism levelled against Percy by later collectors, who objected to his practice of expurgating and editing his original text, Percy's approach to folksong did indeed set the tone for many subsequent folklorists. The ballads and songs in the collection were considered by Percy to be of importance as "rude survivals of the past, deserving of a certain amount of attention as illustrating the language, the numbers, the beliefs and customs of bygone days, although as poetry they had no intrinsic value."[3] Thus almost from the beginning of modern interest in folksong, the seeds of antiquarianism were sown. Folksongs, in this view, were remnants from the past, artifacts of bygone cultures, and their significance for the scholar lay in the glimpse they provided into the mores and attitudes of "primitive" or unenlightened men. It followed also that there was a distinct gap between the rude and clumsy poetry of the folk and the polished verse composed by sophisticated writers. In this too Percy is a precursor of numerous modern folklorists who would not seriously compare folk poetry with the effort of any sophisticated writer. Although there were and are exceptions, folklorists in the nineteenth and twentieth centuries were in general agreement with Percy. Folksong was quaint, curious, of some historical or linguistic interest; but it came to be identified as essentially a thing of the past, a kind of literary fossil which, considering its low origins, was clearly inferior to formal verse.

Herder's response to Percy (and later to the "Ossianic" poems of James Macpherson) needs to be seen in terms of his reaction to the condition of Germany in the eighteenth century. Indeed it was precisely his concern with German nationalism that made him so congenial a figure for Emerson and Whitman during the period which F. O. Matthiessen has so aptly called the "American renaissance." For, unlike England, eighteenth-century Germany was not a nation at all. It consisted of about "eighteen hundred separate territories of various sizes and forms of government, over which an equal number of sovereigns ruled."[4] Economically the country was also disunited, and the situation was worsened by religious feuds and the aftermath of the Thirty Years' War. German literature of the first half of the eighteenth century, moreover, was an imitation of French, Italian, Spanish, and English models. The literary attitudes of the upper classes, in particular, were dominated by the achievements of the French court and of such formidable figures as Molière, Corneille, and Racine.

At the same time, the attitude of Enlightenment thinkers toward cultures of the past was conditioned by what Robert T. Clark, Jr., has called a "caste system in eighteenth-century philosophic anthropology."[5] Only the cultures of Greece, Rome, and France were considered to be of historic importance. Thus the roots of a national culture might be derived from one of these "high" civilizations or, as it turned out in practice, from an intelligentsia steeped in their literary traditions. But it was absurd to suggest that a national culture could be built upon the accomplishments of its own peasantry, especially in Germany or in the countries of eastern Europe, which lay outside the pale of high culture. In fact the idea of acknowledging in any manner the cultural achievements of the lower orders of society ran counter to the major assumptions of enlightenment thinkers. Their conception of cultural progress was predicated upon the eradication of myth and superstition from the minds of the peasantry, whose subjugation by the church prevented them from responding to the new light of rationalist philosophies. Only after this liberation from the heritage of the past could the lower orders of society be raised to the level of educated and rational men. As Clark has noted, this point of view rendered nationalistic movements ridiculous and useless. The lower classes were patently uncivilized, and until they could be purged of their barbaric traditions the Enlightenment viewed them as children of darkness. In any case one could hardly expect to discover the sources of a national literature among them.

Herder's approach to folklore and folksong was in direct opposition to the predilections of Percy as well as to those of the Enlightenment. His work was permeated by one overriding conception, namely, to discover the source for the creation of a distinctly German literary tradition. His identification of that source in the folk traditions of the common people has had immense consequences for social, political, and folkloristic thought in the following two centuries, though his role in developing the idea has often been misunderstood.

Herder's response to Percy's collection is indicative of the position he found himself in. He wrote (and the comment recalls Emerson's plea in *The American Scholar*): "In more than one province I know of folksongs, songs in dialect, peasant songs which, as regards vivacity, and rhythm, simplicity and strength of language, would certainly concede nothing to many of those collected by other nationalities. But who would collect them? Who would trouble himself about the songs of the people on the streets, in alleys and fish markets, in the simple roundelay of the peasant folk, about songs which are often without scansion and with bad rhymes? . . . We would rather read, even though only for pastime, our modern beautifully printed poets."[6] The example of English collectors like Percy was impressive to Herder. But for him the existence of a vital folk tradition was not significant for the light it could throw on the nature of ancient civilizations. He viewed it rather as the means by which Germany could create a unique and characteristic formal literature of its own. Here is one of the central conceptions in Herder's work: the idea that a nation's formal literature needs to be based on the creative accomplishments of its folk, regardless of how crude that body of materials may seem to the sophisticated classes of society.

Almost from the first, therefore, Herder found it necessary to argue for the use of the German language, and this attitude foreshadowed his later conception that the sense of nationality is derived from the unsophisticated folk poetry of the people. A nationality without a language of its own is impossible, he noted, urging Germans to "know your own language . . . and develop it for poetry, philosophy, and prose. For then you are building the foundation which will hold a building." At the same time he pointed out that the idioms of a language are the elements which provide its special character and distinguish it from other languages: "The idioms are the elegances of which no neighbor can deprive us and they are sacred to the tutelary goddess of the language. They are the elegances woven into the spirit of the language, and this spirit is destroyed if they are taken out. . . . Take the idiomatic out of a language and you take its spirit and power. . . . The idioms of the time of the Meistersänger, of Opitz and Logau, of Luther, etc. should be collected. . . . And if they are good for nothing else they will at least open the way to the student of language so he can understand the genius of the nationality, and explain one by the other. The idioms of every language are the impressions of its country, its nationality, its history."[7] The idioms stand in the same relationship to language as the folksongs to formal poetry; in both cases they provide the vitality and spirit which make for a truly national literature.

When Herder applied his views about the sources of national culture to eighteenth-century Germany, the reasons for the lack of a distinctly German tradition in literature were apparent. Owing to the impact of the Renaissance and the Enlightenment, the domination of Latin over the German language, and the subservience of German writers to French literary traditions, Germany had been thwarted from tapping the roots of its own culture. "From ancient times," Herder observed, "we have absolutely no living poetry on which our newer poetry might grow like a branch on the stem. Other nationalities have progressed with the centuries and have built with national products upon a peculiar foundation, with the remains of the past upon the belief and tastes of the *Volk*. In that way their literature and language have become national. The voice of the *Volk* is used and cherished, and in these matters they have cultivated a much larger public than we have. . . . It will remain eternally true that if we have no *Volk*, we shall have no public, no nationality, no literature of our own which shall live and work in us. Unless our literature is founded on our *Volk*, we shall write eternally for closet sages and disgusting critics out of whose mouths and stomachs we shall get back what we have given."[8] The organic images here are significant—indeed we shall encounter them again in Emerson and Whitman in an identical context. What they suggest is the growth of a literary tradition from the lowest levels of the culture to the highest, the latter owing its characteristic form and expression to the underlying roots. Translated into socio-political terms, the ideas reveal the startling assumption that the major literary values of a nation are defined by the lowest strata of the culture. This reverses, of course, the established notion that culture is developed by an elite and then dispersed among the remainder of the people.

As these comments indicate, Herder was operating with a remarkably sophisticated sociological approach. He understood that society was not simply an undifferentiated whole, but rather that it consisted of a dominant culture and subcultures as well. *Volkslied* [folksong] (Herder coined the term in 1771) was the product of a subculture that existed contemporaneously with the dominant one rather than in a distant past. The idea that a subculture might not only contribute to the dominant one, but even define its major outlines was even more startling. At the same time, Herder's formulation marks him not only as *un*antiquarian but also anti-Rousseauvian. For although Rousseau had emphasized the value of "primitive" cultures, he is also responsible for the notion that civilization destroys them. Herder, on the other hand, does not suggest nostalgia for some irretrievable golden age; the importance of his point of view lies in his emphasis upon the persistence within contemporary society of folk traditions and his argument that a national literature can be attained only through building upon them. Later folklorists, especially in Germany and America, often lost sight of this idea, but we shall see how Emerson and Whitman were closer to the spirit of Herder's insight. Folksong was not, for him, the remnant of an antique and outmoded system of values and expression. It spoke directly to the needs of men in their contemporary circumstances.

Herder's concern with the relationship between folklore, folksong, and nationalism has led to a curious misconstruction of his major intentions. Indeed, despite the fact that several excellent studies have appeared in recent years, there is still widespread the notion that Herder is the central source for a racist ideology which has permeated European thought. One reason for this notion is the fact that several generations of folklorists did emphasize the mystical qualities of Teutonic or Anglo-Saxon national essences. And of course it has been difficult to avoid notice of the blatant and brutal excesses of nationalism in Hitler Germany during our own time.

The irony is that Herder's approach to nationalism led him in exactly an opposite direction, away from provincialism or chauvinism. (And it will be important to note that Whitman's reliance on Herder's views provided him also with a check against the excesses of his own nationalistic enthusiasms.) In view of the persisting identification of Herder with chauvinistic ideas, it is worth describing in some detail how his statements about the relationships between folksong and national culture provided him with a principle of historical relativism which clearly prefigures modern anthropological methods. In his major work, *Ideen zur Philosophie der Geschichte der Menschheit,* Herder took strong exception to the Enlightenment notion that the eighteenth century was the apogee of human civilization. "It would be the most stupid vanity," he declared, "to imagine that all the inhabitants of the world must be Europeans to live happily."[9] Every nation has its own unique character and it is not possible to rank one against any other, either in the contemporary world or against the background of ancient history. Herder insisted, however, that the deepest insight into any culture, whether ancient or modern, could be gained by examining its folk tradition. This approach makes every epoch valuable to the historian strictly in its own terms and without regard to the progress of human civilization at any given time. The mind of the primitive may be devoid of sophisticated ideas, Herder acknowledged, "but Nature has conferred another beneficent gift on our species, in leaving to such of its members as are least stored with ideas the first gems of superior sense, exhilarating music . . . and among the most uncultivated nations music is the first of the fine arts, by which every mind is moved. . . . But music, however rude and simple, speaks to every human heart, and this with the dance, constitutes Nature's general festival throughout the earth. Pity it is that most travellers, from too refined a taste, conceal from us those infantile tones of foreign nations. Useless as they may be to the musician, they are instructive to the investigators of man; for the music of a nation, in its most imperfect form and favourite tunes, displays the internal character of the people. . . ."[10] Herder would have been pleased to note how useful folk materials would be to certain kinds of musicians in the nineteenth as well as the twentieth century. (How it came to be used is a subject I will return to.) His concern here is essentially historical and anthropological, and it points directly toward historical and cultural relativism.

Aside from its function of providing the basis for a national literature, folksong revealed to Herder a principle of equality so radical that it is only now beginning to be fully assessed. It suggested that every culture was completely unique in its own right so that there is really no possibility for any normative evaluation or ranking of societies. If the democratic affirmation implicit in Herder's approach is not obvious to modern readers, it is only because, as Clark has observed, "We are living on this side of the French Revolution and the Romantic Movement." In a Germany still bound to the caste system of feudalism, however, Herder's assertion that folksong is the main source of literary value was met with derision and, in religious circles, with charges of blasphemy. Unlike Emerson and other American Herderians, Herder himself was often forced to play down the radical implications of his theory that national literature springs from the folksong created by the lowest orders of society. Yet his very conception of the term *Volk* made the equalitarian turn of Herder's thought apparent. Noting the condescension applied to the word in his time, Herder turned to Ancient Greece (as he conceived of it) for an example of the true meaning of the term. "There," he pointed out, "this name was honorable; it included all citizens except members of the council of priests; now it is synonymous with rabble and *canaille*. There all citizens were equal."[11] In fact, Herder argued, "A folk singer does not have to be from the rabble and sing for the rabble; just as little is the noblest poetry harmed by being sung by the people."[12] On the contrary, according to Herder, it is the folk bard who brings a truly national literature into existence. Yet though each nation creates a distinct literature from its own folk heritage, folk poetry is valuable "because of its constant and international elements."[13]

As Clark has pointed out, several generations of later writers carried nationalism to excesses, "but it would be absurd to attribute that phase to Herder's warmly humane, honestly tolerant national striving."[14] As if to emphasize this element in his thought, Herder's first collection of *Volkslieder* contained not only German folksongs, but examples from Italian, Estonian, Lithuanian, Lettish, Danish, Spanish, Inca, Eskimo, Latin, Greek, and Old Norse. The work is far from satisfying the standards of contemporary folklore or anthropological research; yet it stands as a major instance of Herder's insight into the relationship between national and international values. (Herder's editors changed the title to *Stimmen der Völker in Liedern* [*Voices of the People in Songs*] and the book is best known under that title.) The keystone of his philosophy was the conception of *Humanität*, by which he meant the "harmonious development of all immortal souls toward universally valid goals: reason, freedom, health, finer perceptions, dominion over the earth, the harmonious realisation of all that God has implanted in His noblest work and made in His own image."[15] Hence the idea of racial superiority is explicitly denied by Herder. As one of his recent critics has noted, "it must be remembered that it was not blood but language which Herder regarded as the essential criterion of a *Volk*. *Volk* was conceived as an ethnic and not as a racial community. . . . What is more, the idea of racial superiority, which is the key concept of modern racialism, was completely alien to Herder's mind. He firmly rejected the notion of superman and the idea of master-nations or master-races. Domination or persecution of any kind, whether of man by man, or of one nation by another, was abhorrent to his very being. There is no need to labour the point. Herder, the 'high priest' of *Humanität* was singularly ill-qualified for the part of a precursor of racialist doctrine."[16] This element of internationalism in Herder's thought is indisputable but it has usually been overlooked or even denied, at least in the evaluation of European followers of Herder.

Similarly, the relationship of Herderian thought to American tradition has not been examined closely. Those writers who have considered the impact of Herder on American thinkers have not been dealing, in fact, with Herder's conceptions but rather with their reflection from the work of later German critics and scholars who either vulgarized or distorted his ideology. It is important to note that the heritage of Herderian thought in the United States was extremely close to the letter as well as to the spirit of Herder's authentic views. Why this should be so is difficult to discover, though a good deal of the answer can be found in the general commitment to democratic and equalitarian ideology in the United States. Thus while Herder's views about the roots of a nation's culture were a shock to the sensibilities of many in his own time, they could be readily adapted to the already existing structure and ideology of a nation conceived (at least in theory) on democratic principles.

Before turning to specific analyses of the impact of Herder on American thought, it is worth noting several inferences which could be drawn from his formulations by anyone familiar with his views but which in fact lay dormant until they were extrapolated by American writers. The first and perhaps major issue I have already touched on. It is the simple but insistent argument that the essence of a nation's character as well as its literary expression can be discovered in the folk tradition of its people. Since Herder, that notion has been widely propagated though not so universally acknowledged to be a valid statement. As the principles of democratic institutions were proposed by eighteenth-century thinkers, their justification rested on universal natural rights, to a large extent founded on Lockean theory. Locke's anthropology, however, was essentially prefabricated rather than empirical. He simply assumed that in the state of nature all men had certain basic rights, among them life, liberty, and property. However successful this formulation was (the more so in this country when the last term was changed), it is an excellent example of a circumstance which Alfred North Whitehead has noted in modern thought. In the late middle ages, he points out, the ultimate purpose of prevailing ideology was to assure a commitment to faith, especially in religious thought. But it was based quite fully on rational and logical systems of argument. In the seventeenth and eighteenth centuries the ultimate goal was rationalism, but at crucial points in the arguments of men like Newton and Locke, it became necessary to rely on simple affirmations of faith. As Newton had simply to assume the existence of hard, concrete elements which could be called matter, so also Locke interjected the idea of natural rights on the basis of no empirical data from the history of mankind. Later on of course, Marx and Engels, using the precise data drawn by Lewis Henry Morgan from the social organization of American Indians, punctured the notion that property rights were eternal laws of human existence. In a less obvious manner it has always been possible to attack the notion of equality on the ground that, empirically, men are too often not at all equal. And if the assumptions upon which equalitarian systems rest turn out to be a matter of faith (the belief in a natural rights ideology, for example) then the validity of the entire construct is jeopardized. If we put this in psychological terms it helps to explain what has been a discernible pattern in much liberal thought predicated on Enlightenment assumptions about the equality of man. In the absence of concrete demonstrations that men are equal or that the lower echelons of society have any creative or expressive powers, it is easily possible for the defenders of these assertions to become quickly disillusioned with the common man and find themselves in an elitist or even fiercely antidemocratic frame of mind. The nature of just such a predicament has been the subject matter of much contemporary literature and philosophy, and indeed the result of what has inaccurately been described as Herderian in its origin exposes a similar shift from glorification of the *Volk* to an acceptance of the tyrannical role of the superman.

Herder's position is derived from anti-Lockean and anti-Enlightenment assumptions and moves in an entirely different direction. F. M. Barnard suggests that the deepest nuances of Herder's thought went unnoticed because it was necessary for him often to expurgate the most radical of his views. But whether for the reason that I have already suggested or because the Americans read later texts of his work, they were able to draw the most accurate inferences from his formulations. In particular, Herder provided a major and unique justification for a democratic ideology. It was based on the concrete demonstration of the creative powers of the lower classes. Unlike the Enlightenment argument which assumed a universal law of equality, Herder's folk ideology made it possible to offer empirical proof that the major values of a national literature resided in the abilities of common men to create a folk tradition from which a formal, sophisticated literature developed. This was an argument not easily undermined, for it made it possible to justify the idea of democratic traditions on specific grounds. To use Jefferson's formulation, the existence of folk art provided a major instance of the powers of what he called the "natural aristocracy," based on talent and virtue. The "artificial aristocracy" of birth and money could easily show its accomplishments. But Herder's ideology enabled equalitarian critics to define these accomplishments as derivatives from the germinal and central powers of the folk. Jefferson, of course, could only insist that occasionally the lower classes produced a "diamond in the rough." The Herderian position identified the mine itself. All that was lacking was the collected evidence that a folk tradition existed in this country.

Herder's response to language is another example of how accurately the Americans read him. Isaiah Berlin points out that in opposition to the idea that language was taught to mankind by a specific act of creation, Herder believed that "language was an intrinsic part of the natural process of the growth of consciousness, indeed of human solidarity, which rests on the communication between men; for to be fully human is to think, and to think is to communicate; society and man are equally inconceivable without one another. Hence, 'mere intelligence without the expression of language is on earth a mere utopia.' Herder means that it is inconceivable rather than improbable. Words, by connecting passions with things, the present with the past, and by making possible memory and imagination, create family, society, literature, history. He declares that to speak and think in words is to 'swim in an inherited stream of words; we must accept these media on trust: we cannot create them.' "[17] We recall that the creation of a language is essentially the accomplishment of the folk; it is a legacy that the sophisticated members of a society inherit though they do not always acknowledge that it is what makes them human.

But if language alone makes it possible to conceptualize experience, in its written form it also freezes it. And although Berlin notes that Herder never reconciled this contradiction, he has helped us to understand the attraction of folk tradition to a mind like Herder's. Oral tradition provides a constant pressure against what Herder calls "linguistic petrification." Berlin argues that the "history of linguistic revolutions is the history of the succession of cultures, the true revolutions in the history of the human race." Primitive poetry is essentially magical and "a spur to action—to heroes, hunters, lovers; it stimulates and directs. It is not to be savoured by the scholar in his armchair, but is intelligible only to those who have placed themselves in situations similar to the conditions in which such words sprang into existence." For Herder, in short, folk tradition is the agent for accomplishing linguistic change and, beyond that, for revolutionizing the cultural values of society. Folklorists, on the other hand, have generally noted that the folk process itself is a conservative activity. In opposition to what often occurs in popular culture or in formal literature, it has been demonstrated that the folk does not easily give up its traditions, which evolve slowly and imperceptibly over long periods of time. If the process of folk development is essentially conservative, how can we explain the tendency in American thought to use folklore as a justification for social change or protest?

Several answers to this question will be provided by our study of Emerson, Whitman, Constance Rourke, and the Lomaxes. But a main clue is provided by noting that a radical strategy was developed by Herder through an ideological position based on his analysis of the function of folk tradition within a given culture. This is a corollary of his main conception that folklore is the source of a national literature. It follows then that folk tradition may also provide a measure for the vitality of an existing literary approach, just as a fresh source may constantly maintain the health and vitality of the superstructure created upon it—and it is this view that I define as folk ideology. It is notable also that "the corruption of man is followed by the corruption of language. When the simplicity of character and the sovereignty of ideas is broken up by the prevalence of secondary desires —the desire of riches, of pleasure, of power, and of praise—and duplicity and falsehood take the place of simplicity and truth, the power over nature as an interpreter of the will is lost; new imagery ceases to be created, and old words are perverted to stand for things which are not; a paper currency is employed, when there is no bullion in the vaults. In due time the fraud is manifest, and words lose all power to stimulate the understanding or the affections." Thus the revolutionary power of language is made manifest—but this is not Herder; it is Emerson in *Nature*.

In fact Herder's conception of the scholar out in the world, reviving his sensibilities by contact with active and working men is so close an approximation to Emerson's view of the American Scholar as to demand here only passing notice. Emerson, as we shall see, had many sources for developing his own views along these lines, and although there is no doubt that Herder must be counted among them, the matter of influences is my last concern. Nevertheless it is significant that what Emerson and other American writers responded to in Herder's thought was largely overlooked by Herder's immediate followers. Berlin has noted that there is a conception of individualism in Herder which is "closer to the anarchism of Thoreau or Proudhon or Kropotkin . . . than to the ideals of Fichte or Hegel or political socialists. . . . He stands with those who protest against mechanization and vulgarisation rather than with the nationalists of the last hundred years, whether moderate or violent."[18] Berlin's formulation of this principle in Herder's thought is "the equal validity of incommensurable cultures," a notion which he finds even more threatening to the traditional structures of Western thought than that developed by Hume. So radical a principle makes it impossible to judge any culture by the standards of another; but more important it places the "primitive mind" and the folk art whereby it is expressed on an equal level with the accomplishments of "sophisticated society."[19]

It is precisely this aspect of Herder's philosophy that has special relevance for American thought which, from the beginning, has had the label of savagery pinned on it, in derogatory as well as in honorific contexts. Above all it brings to mind that peculiar form of American anarchism founded upon the awareness that the individual personality is the result of a continuing communal source: the individual is all, yet his culture has been shaped by processes that can only be understood in terms of the anonymous movement of the folk. The attempts to control this delicate balance between the individual and the mass have often exhibited what seems to be a major inconsistency in American thought, an inconsistency that seems to stem from our cultural immaturity; and our writers have reacted to such intimations with a variety of strategies which I propose to discuss in detail. Whitman's remains the most characteristic formulation: "Do I contradict myself?/ Very well then I contradict myself,/ (I am large, I contain multitudes.)" Often the American writer employed a comic technique which we shall encounter regularly in which an American character fully accepts the stereotypes developed by Europeans, playing to the hilt the role of barbarian, all the while poking fun at the credulity of his critics. But underlying this is a serious commitment to the idea that civilization (specifically the inherited civilization of the Old World) is a static and lifeless entity which needs the fertile powers of folk culture to bring it back to life. The recurring affronts to the "establishment" in our literature as well as in our politics are testimony to the persistence of this approach. Herder's idea of the equal validity of incommensurable cultures operates not only in terms of the relationships among nations; it appears as an ideological force within American culture itself.

We can begin to see why folkloristic arguments appear in writers who otherwise seem not to have been concerned with folklore itself. In a society which has been forced to identify itself as "a nation of nations," the attempt to provide absolute definitions is seriously undermined, and a folk ideology such as I have been describing lies close at hand to aid in the subversion. Hence while we shall note arguments in support of the unity of American culture, it will be demonstrable that a central tradition of diversity and philosophical anarchism exists as well. This is particularly evident in the tendencies of the writers and scholars under discussion here to define the characteristic American expression as the result of hybridization rather than as pure ethnic entities. And like most germinal American thinkers, they are suspicious of traditional categories of description and systems of classification in general. As Perry Miller has pointed out, the only generalization one can make about the American character is an ironic one: "he who would fix the pattern of decision by confining the American choice to one and only one mode of response—whether this be in politics, diplomacy, economics, literary form, or morality itself—such a one, in the light of our history, is the truly 'Un-American.' "[20]

Few critics have examined closely the relationships between folk ideology and literary theory in the United States from the nineteenth century to the present time. Nor have they noticed the adaptation and development of what I shall describe as Herderian formulations in the context of American conditions. Yet major attempts to define the sources of an American literary tradition have persistently been based on approaches strikingly similar to those first suggested by Herder. These include the emphasis on folklore as a foundation for national culture; the effort to provide a legitimacy for American English (and vernacular diction) as well as the reaction against the subservience to European (and especially British) tradition; the use of folk ideology as a means of balancing a fundamentally individualistic and anarchistic tradition with the sense of collective responsibilities; and finally, the essential commitment to a society open to the salutary influences of folk traditions. In all these areas there is a Herderian thread that runs through the speculations of several generations of American writers and scholars. But it is worth reiterating that the relationships between Herder's ideas and American thought go far beyond the matter of influences. Herder's views seemed eminently appropriate to American conditions, and writers in this country often pushed them to extremes. This is one of innumerable instances in which Americans have adapted European sources to serve their own needs; but since there is so often an independent development of similar views, I think it likely that if Herder had not existed, the Americans would have invented him.

Chapter Two

The Emerson-Whitman Tradition: Emerson

IN ONE of his rare comments on Britain's American colonies Herder wrote: "Perhaps when the arts and sciences shall have become decadent in Europe, they will arise there with new blossoms, with new fruit." But even Herder would have been surprised to know what fertile soil his conceptions would find in this country. Herder's ideas were known in America as early as the first decade of the nineteenth century and the continuing interest in his work may be attested to by the essay on Herder which George Bancroft published in the *North American Review* in 1825, as well as by translations and articles which appeared in popular magazines. One of the main sources of information about Herder's religious thought was James Marsh's translation of *The Spirit of Hebrew Poetry* in 1833. Henry A. Pochmann notes that Marsh's book inspired George Ripley's "Life of Herder," which ran for fifty-six pages in the *Christian Examiner*.[1] Interest in Herder continued and was heightened by the publication in 1841 of the New York edition of T. O. Churchill's translation of Herder's *Ideen* (London, 1800). The publication of the *Ideen* aroused much interest in America, but it was to the Transcendentalists that he seemed to speak most directly. Of particular interest was Herder's exegesis of biblical texts, and the German's reputation is indicated by the comment of Calvin E. Stowe, who wrote in 1829: "If you would ascertain the great principles on which you must judge of the Hebrew poetry, and become acquainted with its characteristic features, study Lowth; if you desire to know more of the precise idea which the Hebrew poets intend to express, and to trace with philological accuracy the sources of their language and imagery, follow the criticism of Michaelis; but if you would lay aside the philosopher and critic and give yourself up to intellectual enjoyment, if you would have the same sensations and the same thoughts, while chanting the Hebrew poetry, which the ancient Hebrews themselves had, catch the tuneful notes of Herder."[2] Marsh's translation is known to have been a favorite with Emerson and his aunt, Mary Moody Emerson, but as early as 1824 Emerson's brother, William, had written from Germany: "Read all of Herder you can get." And in 1829 Emerson borrowed from the Harvard College Library Churchill's translation of the *Ideen*.[3]

Emerson's attraction to Herder was twofold: on the one hand he was impressed by Herder's organic theory of the relationship between man and nature and the humanistic theology which developed from it; on the other hand, Herder's concern with the question of nationalism could not but be congenial to the mind of Emerson during the period of the "American renaissance." Although the main thrust of this literary nationalism reveals many Herderian parallels, Emerson nevertheless remained stubbornly independent and original in his formulations. As Stephen Whicher has noted: "When all allowance is made for sources, Emerson's position remains substantially a fresh insight of his own, whose nature he worked out initially by inspection without much regard to precedent."[4] His reliance on a folk ideology to define the nature of an American literary tradition developed quite naturally from his deep commitments to equalitarian thought; indeed we shall encounter echoes of this element of Emerson's thought in the work of Constance Rourke and the Lomaxes. As early as 1826 Emerson had written in his *Journals,* "Ballads, bon mots, anecdotes, give us better insights into the depths of past centuries than grave and voluminous chronicles"; and in *Nature* (1836) he emphasized the germinal power of folk speech: "Because of this radical correspondence between visible things and human thoughts, savages, who have only what is necessary, converse in figures. As we go back in history, language becomes more picturesque, until its infancy, when it is all poetry; or all spiritual facts are represented by natural symbols. . . . It has moreover been observed, that the idioms of all languages approach each other in passages of the greatest eloquence and power. *And as this is the first language, so is it the last."* [my italics]. Some of Emerson's most shocking comments are best understood within the context of his view that folk tradition is a source for the rejuvenation of effete literary conventions. "Not out of those on whom systems of education have exhausted their culture," he argued in *The American Scholar,* "comes the helpful giant to destroy the old or build the new, but out of unhandselled savage nature; out of terrible druids and Berserkers come at last Alfred and Shakespeare." And when he listed in "The Poet" a catalogue of subjects for the American bard he included prominently Negroes and Indians as an appropriate source of materials.

The political implications of Emerson's ideology, however, have been fully explored. I am more concerned with an esthetic formulation in Emerson's thought which made it possible to use the resources of folk tradition in such a way as to avoid merely reproducing archaic forms. Even more important is the fact that his analysis led him to a position which is strikingly contemporary and closely related to the speculations on the same subject by James Joyce, whose theory of "epiphanies" has received a good deal of critical attention. Emerson's position, on the other hand, is too often overwhelmed by the political or sociological issues which, it must be admitted, occupied a good portion of his writing and extraliterary activities. But in *Nature,* his first major work, Emerson developed a theory of literature which has the closest affinities to contemporary literary concerns.

In the introduction Emerson raises the questions which he proposes to investigate and, although they clearly carry overtones of political and regional issues, the central query is: "Why should not we have a poetry and philosophy of insight and not of tradition, and a religion by revelation to us, and not the history of theirs?" The last reference is to "foregoing generations," and as Perry Miller has pointed out, the Transcendentalists' resistance to the New England heritage (especially that of Unitarianism) was "nothing less than the first of a succession of revolts by the youth of America against American philistinism."[5] (It is obviously an early manifestation of what we now call the generation gap.) Emerson's main concern, however, is with poetry, philosophy, and religion, and his quest is for a theory of nature which will "explain all phenomena." At present, he notes, "many are thought not only unexplained, but inexplicable; as language, sleep, madness, dreams, beasts, sex." Emerson's penchant for catalogues often leads him to promise more than he is capable of making good. Of the subjects named, the key item is language, for it is in his conception of the function and meaning of language that Emerson is most provocative. Indeed, in the over-all scheme of *Nature* (including the introduction) the section on language is precisely at the center of the book. Emerson's discussion, however, has too often been patronized by scholars who have made the most of some questionable generalizations. He states, for example: "Every word which is used to express a moral or intellectual fact, if traced to its roots, is found to be borrowed from some material appearance." That kind of literal-mindedness is rare in Emerson, who is generally attacked for his muddleheadedness. His main point in the section, however, is clear: "It is not words only that are emblematic; it is things which are emblematic . . . man is an analogist, and studies relations in all objects." Emerson's formula for explaining this notion is well known, but I want to reproduce it here in order to take a fresh look at it:

1. Words are signs of natural facts.

2. Particular natural facts are symbols of particular spiritual facts.
3. Nature is a symbol of spirit.

The connection between mind and matter, Emerson explains, "is not fancied by some poet, but stands in the will of God, and so is true to be known by all men. It appears to men or it does not appear." It is the occurrence of these appearances that interests Emerson, and in a famous passage he describes what he later calls "the best moments of life . . . these delicious awakenings of the higher powers." He recalls an occasion when, "Crossing a bare common, in snow puddles, at twilight, under a clouded sky, without having in my thoughts any occurrence of special good fortune, I have enjoyed a perfect exhilaration. I am glad to the brink of fear. . . . Standing on the bare ground—my head bathed by the blithe air and uplifted into infinite space—all mean egotism vanishes. I become a transparent eyeball; I am nothing; I see all; the currents of the universal Being circulate through me; I am part or parcel of God." Faced with so extreme a statement of mysticism, many of Emerson's readers have too often simply registered the main outlines of his position and then moved on to passages less abstruse. To be sure, Emerson needs to be viewed in the context of a mystical tradition that reaches back to Jonathan Edwards (if not to seventeenth-century Puritanism itself), and which foreshadows the characteristic thought of William James.

But it is Emerson's analysis of the sources of these "delicious awakenings" and his prescriptions for their evocation that need to be looked at closely. Here he is less a provincial mystic than the formulator of a major literary esthetic which has had wide influence here and abroad. It would be well to keep in mind the elements in Emerson's formula: there is, at first, the *opaque* eyeball, which is the gateway to the mind. The mind perceives language, which emanates from the natural facts of the material world. If these two are in the proper relation, then the channels open and the underlying spiritual truths come into focus, resulting in the "delicious awakening," which Emerson identifies with the image of the *transparent* eyeball. In this formulation, language (words) and the natural facts are fixed and necessary stages in the process whereby the spiritual truths may be revealed. As Emerson gives it, the creative process is by definition an indirect one, with language and the natural facts as intermediaries which must be passed through to achieve the heightened consciousness of those "best moments of life."

Yet for all his vaunted optimism, Emerson insists that "A man is a god in ruins. . . . Man is the dwarf of himself. Once he was permeated and dissolved by spirit. He filled nature with his overflowing currents." In an earlier time, that is to say, man's connection with the world of spirit was direct, the spiritual truths flowing from their source to his mind without intermediaries. Emerson seems to have in mind an Adamic state, when God spoke directly to man, whose innocence may be defined by precisely this instinctive and immediate relationship to the spiritual world. But that path has been blocked and though Emerson does not put it in these terms, it is a clear analogy to man's fall from grace; his sin has deprived him of the ability to find communion purely and without intermediaries or conscious effort. "The ruin or the blank that we see when we look at nature," Emerson says, "is in our own eye. The axis of vision is not coincident with the axis of things, and so they appear not transparent but opaque." In the Adamic condition, one can speculate, there was no poetic expression as such because man's existence was so closely attuned to the world of spirit as to be poetic in its every manifestation. It is a situation reminiscent of the circumstances in Eden regarding sex before the fall: before their transgression Adam and Eve seemed unaware of sex, yet they may be assumed to have indulged in it with that unconsciousness of the lower animals. (It brings to mind D. H. Lawrence's notion that the fall is best defined as the consciousness of sexual guilt which develops after Adam and Eve have eaten of the forbidden fruit.) Similarly, in Emerson's version of Eden, Adam and Eve were "natural" artists.

Although the direct source of communion is broken, certain small sparks may still flicker across the gap, quite unexpectedly and with no conscious effort, as in the passage quoted earlier wherein Emerson becomes a "transparent eyeball." The effect is to stimulate the Reason, which Emerson describes as a property of the mind that controls the creative faculty and which is cognate with the main character of the spiritual world. In his fallen state, however, man relies on the Understanding, which is simply a faculty for dealing with surface realities: "The understanding adds, divides, combines, measures, and finds nutriment and room for its activity in this worthy scene [that is, in Nature]. Meantime, Reason transfers all these lessons to its own world of thought, by perceiving the analogy that marries Matter and Mind." As we shall see, Emerson promises that in his right state man should operate with both the Understanding and Reason. But it is the latter that occasionally stirs men into an awareness of their full power, and we would probably be accurate in describing the process through this route as inspiration, which unpredictably flashes across the broken circuit, though Emerson insists that the occurrence takes place in the presence of Nature.

Under present circumstances, however, spiritual consciousness is more likely to take another route, functioning through two intermediaries: language and natural facts. It is therefore distinct from the inspirational route, first because it is not direct, and second because it is not unconscious. The notion of indirection is important in several ways, but mainly it reveals how perceptive Emerson's speculations about language were. His position is consciously anti-Lockean: it is not brute sensation that man perceives, but words, which are themselves the symbols of natural facts. Like a number of contemporary philosophers, Emerson tends to identify man and to distinguish him from the lower animals by his symbol-making faculties. What man knows comes to him in symbolic form, through the medium of language, and this is true of all men in all societies. But if Emerson insists on the definition of man as a symbolist, he is equally insistent on the necessity for the symbols to devolve from natural facts.

Perhaps the best way to explain Emerson's attitude is to examine the rather distinct form of philosophical idealism which it represents. Emerson is usually described as a pantheist, though the word is rarely defined. And though pantheism carries as many meanings as the writers who use it, it often denotes the idea that nature is the essential manifestation of god. Emerson's attitude toward nature, however, is not pantheistic in this sense of the word. As his formula indicates, nature is one of the two intermediaries between man and the world of spirit, which has its own precise designation. "Nature is the symbol of spirit," Emerson says, and "The imagination may be defined to be the use which Reason makes of the material world." Until the "eye of Reason opens," nature seems to be absolute, but when the imagination begins to operate, "outlines and surfaces become transparent, and are no longer seen; causes and spirits are seen through them." These are the best moments of life, "the reverential withdrawing of nature before its God." This is perhaps the closest one can come to a definition of Transcendentalism: the "transfiguration which all material objects undergo through the passion of the poet." But unlike traditional idealism, Emerson's version insists stubbornly on the existence and the function of the natural world. Organized religion, he says, degrades nature: "It does that for the unschooled, which philosophy does for Berkeley and Viasa. The uniform language that may be heard in the churches of the most ignorant sects is—'Contemn the unsubstantial shows of the world; they are vanities, dreams, shadows, unrealities; seek the realities of religion.' The devotee flouts nature. Some theosophists have arrived at a certain hostility and indignation towards matter, as the Manicheans and Plotinus. They distrusted in themselves any looking back to these flesh pots of Egypt. Plotinus was ashamed of his body. In short, they might all say of matter what Michael Angelo said of external beauty, 'It is the frail and weary weed, in which God dresses the soul which he has called into time.'" Emerson, on the other hand, has "no hostility to nature, but a child's love to it. I expand and live in the warm day like corn and melons. Let us speak her fair. I do not wish to fling stones at my beautiful mother, nor soil my gentle nest." Although on occasion Emerson seems to attribute godhood to nature, he consistently returns to the notion of its intermediary position between man and God. It is "faithful to the cause whence it had its origin. It always speaks of Spirit. It suggests the absolute. It is a perpetual effect. It is a great shadow pointing always to the sun behind us." Nature is "the apparition of God," "the world is a divine dream," "a remoter and inferior incarnation of God, a projection of God in the unconscious." Finally, it is "the present expositor of the divine mind." Nature then is "thoroughly mediate," and epitomizes the basically symbolic mode of man's perception. Always at one remove from the ultimate spirit, nature is nevertheless a concrete reality and a crucial element in the process whereby man finds a relationship with God. Natural facts are symbols of spirit, language symbolizes or translates the natural facts into the medium man can comprehend, and "every object rightly seen unlocks a new faculty of the soul."

As Emerson explains in "The Poet," the function of the artist is to find the correct word which will begin the sequence I have described above, producing the moment of ecstasy and enlightenment. In *Nature* Emerson emphasizes the "occasional examples of the action of man upon nature with his entire force—with reason as well as understanding." Both are clearly necessary to achieve the moments of "instantaneous instreaming causing power." The yoking of the Understanding and the Reason is another instance of Emerson's "trascendental materialism," his insistence that the realm of matter plays a major role in man's awareness of spiritual truths. "The invariable mark of wisdom is to see the miraculous in the common," he maintains. In the following comment we can see most clearly the implications of Emerson's view for the practice of poetry: "What is a day? What is a year? What is summer? What is woman? What is a child? What is sleep? To our blindness, these things seem unaffecting. We make fables to hide the baldness of the fact and conform it, as we say, to the higher law of the mind. But when the fact is seen under the light of an idea, the gaudy fable fades and shrivels. We behold the real higher law. To the wise, therefore, a fact is true poetry, and the most beautiful of fables. . . . Whilst the abstract question occupies your intellect, nature brings it in the concrete to be solved by your hands." The poet works by indirection through the symbolism of language, but he needs also to be rooted in concrete reality, which is the second requirement in the attempt to make a connection with the realm of spirit. Though its end is transcendent, poetry lives through the material and, as Emerson indicates, its language will reflect the concreteness of ordinary diction and commonplace subjects; which is to say, that in this formulation Emerson's political folk ideology and his esthetic principles come together, the one consonant with the other. At bottom, of course, Emerson is describing a mystical process and though one can argue about its validity it seems to me unprofitable. Emerson posits a mystical belief and the reader can take it or leave it. Given the extreme limitations of our understanding of how language functions, we are not likely to arrive at any definitive conclusions. But we should not miss the esthetic and historical implications of Emerson's theory of creativity on that account.

Emerson's esthetic is aimed essentially at producing that moment of ecstasy in which a higher spiritual and emotional truth is perceived. The poet accomplishes this through a calculated use of language, which is to say through a symbolist method. In this context, symbolism means the presentation of meaning through the agency of highly metaphorical language, rather than in an expository mode of discourse. In "The Poet" Emerson explains that, "Theologians think it a pretty air-castle to talk of the spiritual meaning of a ship or a cloud, of a city or a contract, but they prefer to come again to the solid ground of historical evidence; and even poets are contented with a civil and conformed manner of living, and to write poems from the fancy, at a safe distance from their own experience. But the highest minds of the world have never ceased to explore the double meaning, or shall I say the quadruple or the centruple or much more manifold meaning of every sensuous fact." The virtue of the indirect as opposed to the direct statement (what Emerson refers to as "historical") is precisely its ability to carry the multiple meanings which poetic language can convey. At the same time, the poet must derive his symbols from the sensuous facts of nature: "Nature offers all her creatures to him as picture-language. Being used as a type, a second wonderful value appears in the object, far better than its old value; as the carpenter's stretched cord if you hold your ear close enough, is musical in the breeze. 'Things more excellent than every image,' says Jamblichus, 'are expressed through images.' Things admit of being used as symbols because nature is a symbol, in whole, and in every part." The combination of a symbolic mode of discourse and the emphasis upon the concrete facts from which the language emanates are the main marks of Emerson's esthetic, though the implications of his approach have been too often neglected. In part this is because Emerson's poetry too rarely reflects his esthetic philosophy and in this respect he is like Edgar Allan Poe, although the latter's conceptions have received greater appreciation despite the disparity between his theory and practice.

Indeed much of what has been said about Poe's symbolist approach can be related closely to the views of Emerson, and I would argue that Emerson's conceptions are more relevant to an understanding of America's poetic tradition. In a consideration of Poe's influence on three generations of French poets, for example, T. S. Eliot has provided some major clues to the difference in attitude of the American and European appreciators of Poe.[6] Baudelaire, Mallarmé, and Valéry each responded to separate elements in Poe's legacy; for Baudelaire it was the image of the poet as rebel and outcast, for Mallarmé it was Poe's interest in the technique of verse. Valéry, however, prized above all Poe's idea that "the subject is little, the treatment is everything." Eliot quotes Baudelaire's remark along the same line (poetry "should have nothing in view but itself") though he points out that it was Valéry who made the most of the idea. It leads, of course, to the conception of *la poesie pure*. Pure poetry, Eliot explains, depends on an attitude toward the subject matter: "The subject exists for the poem, not the poem for the subject." Moreover, for Valéry the center of interest is not the poem at all, but the processes of its author as he brings it into being. Even art for art's sake was too great a commitment for Valéry, whose skepticism was so extreme as to preclude "refuge in a doctrine of 'art for art's sake.'"

With Valéry we get a sense of the immense possibilities of symbolism in language, and the fascination of the poet with his own processes of creation, so much so that, as Eliot points out, Valéry often described his poems as "rough drafts," having lost interest in the ends of poetry. These are views which may be found in all three poets, and Eliot confesses that the two main attitudes which he believes derive from Poe (that the poem should have nothing in view but itself, and that the act of composition "is more interesting than the poem which results from it") have brought into existence much of the modern poetry which he admires and enjoys. But significantly, Eliot cannot himself accept the notion of pure poetry. In a primitive state, he explains, "the attention of the listener is directed upon the subject matter," and is not fully aware of the poetic art. At a second stage, when a consciousness of language developed, the listener, who may also have become a reader as well, "is aware of a double interest in a story for its own sake, and in the way in which it is told; that is to say, he becomes aware of style." And in a final stage, the subject matter may exist only as a means of accomplishing the poem itself. Then, Eliot points out, "the reader or listener may become as nearly indifferent to the subject matter as the primitive listener was to the style. A complete unconsciousness or indifference to the style at the beginning, or to the subject matter at the end, would however take us outside of poetry altogether: for a complete unconsciousness of anything but style would mean that poetry had vanished." Poetry, he argues, "is only poetry so long as it preserves some 'impurity' in this sense: that is to say, so long as the subject matter is valued for its own sake."

Although Eliot was unwilling to follow to its logical conclusion the "extreme awareness of and concern for language" which characterizes Valéry's philosophy, he could not keep himself from valuing "this exploration of certain poetic possibilities for its own sake, as we believe that all possibilities should be explored." But like many American poets he found its general assumptions untenable for his own art. It seems curious then that he was not inclined to pay some attention to Emerson's esthetic, which is in fact much closer to his own position. It provides for the same emphasis on symbolism and the possibilities of language and often reproduces that sense of the magical in poetry which Eliot admires in the French. For although Emerson's poet can articulate what other men cannot, words are still at two removes from spiritual truths and there is in his position a tentativeness not far from Valéry's. Emerson asserts that "poems are a corrupt version of some text in nature with which they ought to be made to tally." But as we have seen, the resort to symbolism is a measure of man's separation from the world of spirit and despite his reliance on the possibility of communion through the practice of poetry, it is at best an outline or a sketch of the ultimate connection between man and God: "But lest I should mislead any when I have my own head and obey my whims, let me remind the reader that I am only an experimenter. Do not set the least value on what I do, or the least discredit on what I do not, as if I pretended to settle any thing as true or false. I unsettle all things. No facts to me are sacred; none are profane; I simply experiment, an endless seeker with no past at my back." That could be Whitman, or any one of a number of contemporary American poets, or even Valéry speaking, but it is Emerson, in his essay, "Circles."

Yet despite these tendencies, Emerson holds tenaciously to the idea that the natural facts play an essential part in the production of poetry, insisting on just those "impurities" which Eliot found indispensable to the existence of poetry. "The thought and the form are equal in the order of time," he says in "The Poet," "but in the order of genesis the thought is prior to the form." The true inspiration of the poet is not attained through wines or opiates but results from "the ravishment of the intellect by coming nearer to the fact." The difference between the poet and the mystic, he argues, is "that the last nails a symbol to one sense, which was a true sense for a moment, but soon becomes old and false. For all symbols are fluxional; all language is vehicular and transitive, and is good as ferries and horses are, for conveyance, not as farms and houses are, for homestead." Consistently Emerson proposes an esthetic which values the symbolism of language but retains also a sense of the subject matter for its own sake.

Eliot never acknowledged the affinity between Emerson's philosophy of composition and his own preferences because, for one thing, the political implications of Emerson's views were too far from Eliot's ideological commitments. Indeed we shall see that Eliot operates with his own folk ideology though it does not lead to an affirmation of equalitarian tradition.

In fact, Eliot draws from it an elitist conception of the function of poetry. Yet he greatly admired James Joyce's literary theories, which I suggest are very close to Emerson's. Joyce's theory of epiphanies was his prescription for eliciting those delicious moments of illumination which are the apogee of artistic creation. His only discussion of the theory appears in the first draft of *A Portrait of the Artist as a Young Man,* which has been published under the title, *Stephen Hero.*[7] Overhearing the fragment of a conversation between a young man and a young woman, Stephen was led to "think of collecting many such moments together in a book of epiphanies. By an epiphany he meant a sudden spiritual manifestation, whether in the vulgarity of speech or gesture or in a memorable phase of the mind itself. He believed that it was for the man of letters to record these epiphanies with extreme care, seeing that they themselves are the most delicate and evanescent moments. . . . Imagine my glimpse at the clock [he explains to his skeptical friend Cranly] as the gropings of a spiritual eye which seeks to adjust its vision to an exact focus. The moment the focus is reached the object is epiphanised. . . . The soul of the commonest object, the structure of which is so adjusted, seems to us radiant. The object achieves its epiphany."[8] Joyce's spiritual eye is like Emerson's transparent eyeball, and for both the natural fact is indispensable to the process.

Emerson's epiphanies are admittedly on the level of theory and discussion rather than in the practice of his poetry. Yet it is clear that Emerson had just such a notion of epiphanies as we find in Joyce. F. O. Matthiessen, for example, quotes the following passage from Emerson: "Day creeps after day, each full of facts, dull, strange, despised things, that we cannot enough despise,—call heavy, prosaic and desert. The time we seek to kill: the attention it is elegant to divert from things around us. And presently the aroused intellect finds gold and gems in one of these scorned facts,—then finds that the day of facts is a rock of diamonds; that a fact is an Epiphany of God."[9] Joyce moved in the opposite direction, to the chagrin of his critics, for after this brief description he implemented the theory without further elaboration. (It is mentioned once briefly in *Ulysses* and the passage on epiphanies was omitted from the final text of *A Portrait.*) Yet it should be added that in *Ulysses* Joyce was much concerned with folk tradition and in *Finnegans Wake* he became even more obsessed with the heritage of myth and folklore as a context for his own language experiments.[10] Emerson's esthetic laid the ground for a major approach in American literature which enabled later writers to develop the possibilities of folk tradition and at the same time push the implications of language to its highest level. The resources of American speech could be unleashed as an affront against genteel proprieties, thus fulfilling the requirements for a national literature. In the process, and as a result of Emerson's insights into the nature of symbolism, a literary form emerged which was in the mainstream of esthetic developments.

The difficulty with Emerson as a poet, however, can be seen if we apply his esthetic principles to his own poetry. One of his great virtues, as I have already suggested, was his ability to identify what needed to be done in order to bring an American literature into being. But that did not guarantee that it could be implemented and hence Emerson is much better as a critic than as a poet. But even here Emerson is in the vanguard of literary techniques, for like a good many contemporary writers, he often attempts to use the poem as a way of stating esthetic principles. His esthetic, however, is never very far from his political ideology and this may help us to understand the difficulties that some of his critics have in evaluating his achievement. A recent evaluation of his work provides a valuable insight into a ques-

tion which has been at the center of most discussions of American literature, and since it is one which will interest me considerably, it is worth
identifying it in some detail. In his analysis of Emerson's approach,
Tony Tanner has noted Emerson's obsession with the particular fact
and points out that it can be understood in connection with the overall movement in American literature toward the use of a vernacular
diction: "But the implications of this attitude are worth pondering. If
every fact is equally interesting where does one find a criteria of ex-
clusion, a principle of abridgement without which art cannot start to
be art for it cannot leave off being nature? Emerson is endorsing an
eye which refuses to distinguish and classify, which denies priorities
of importance and significance, which refuses to admit of any sort of
difference in import and value. From one point of view one could call
this the egalitarian eye: an eye which affirms the equality of all facts.
All facts are born equal and have an equal claim on man's attention."[11] It leads Tanner to the major question, for he points out that in
"most art there is what we might call an aristocratic tendency: a
claimed prerogative to exercise a lordly right of selection, omission,
evaluation, and rearrangement." Tanner is aware of the power of the
naive eye, but he is concerned about the problem of form, the possibilities for organizing perception so that it will control the complexity
and "density of experience." In an older culture, there is a mediating
tradition which will help to contain this tendency toward diffusion, but
like most American writers Emerson has no tradition to lean on; he
is "a man talking metaphysics with his eye glued to the microscope."
The result is that while Emerson can be seen as a major liberating force
in American tradition, he develops a style "that stops before society
and the problems of human behavior start."

It is tempting to relate this to the notion developed by Berlin in connection with Herder. We might agree with Tanner that what Emerson
has spawned is a conception of the equal validity of incommensurable
facts, a radical psychology that suddenly begins to suggest the approaches of our most modern writers. But my own analysis of Emerson's esthetic suggests several sources of disagreement with Tanner.
For while Emerson's application of this approach does often result in
seemingly unrelated collections of facts, both he and Whitman were
capable of constructing a usable form on the basis of Emerson's insights into the nature of language. If I have been correct in my estimate of Emerson's approach to epiphany, then there is more meaning
in his assertion that "bare lists of words are found to be suggestive to
an imaginative and excited mind" than most critics have been willing
to acknowledge. For that is precisely what Whitman was capable of

showing in the remarkable catalogues of "Song of Myself." Moreover, we miss an essential element of Emerson's approach if we underestimate (as I believe Tanner does) the sophistication of Emerson's evaluation of symbolism in language. The sense of concreteness is only significant for him if it is seen in the context of language and the spiritual truths which then may be epiphanized. Hence we have indeed something like an egalitarianism in language, but it can only be understood as an outgrowth of the democratic ideology which we have also noted in Emerson's work. It means in effect that the lowest levels of diction, concrete and vulgar as they may appear to respectable society, contain possibilities for the highest level of expression. I think Emerson's major contribution lies in providing both the ideology and the esthetic for justifying that view, which speaks also to the issue that Tanner has raised concerning the asocial tendencies of Emerson's philosophy. Actually Emerson's anarchism is, like most expressions of extreme individualism in this country, always the other side of a position which is much aware of the communal nature of organized society. I have tried to emphasize this by placing Emerson's views in the context of Herder's folk ideology, which should help us to understand that however enthusiastic Emerson could be about the powers of the individual poet, he saw him also as the founder of a national culture and the inheritor of a legacy in language that encompasses all mankind. But he insisted that each nation had its own unique contribution to make, and he believed that the American poet was on the safest ground when he stayed close to the language of his own common people. Given the universal powers of language and symbolism, he was convinced that an appropriate form would emerge that would satisfy the needs of American conditions. Placed in this context, the organic principle becomes the most revolutionary of Emerson's conceptions. An accurate assessment of the nature of American experience, he averred, would result in a unique expression capable of containing it. This is not an aversion to form, but the insistence that the form of American literature must be a radical departure from the forms of other countries—each of which will be valid in its own terms. This is essentially Herderian; what is strictly Emerson's is the proposal of an esthetic that will make it possible. And as that esthetic was used by Whitman, it revealed itself to be a truly radical and impressive source of formal organization.

Emerson's applications, however, are on the whole disappointing. In the case of a poem such as "Uriel," for example, he seems entirely to have forgotten the necessity of just that sense of concrete natural facts which he identified as a major source of epiphanic vision. The poem is usually discussed in the context of Emerson's fall from prestige subsequent to his delivery of the "Divinity School Address." Uriel, the young rebel is overheard dispensing heresy to the young gods who are apparently Platonic philosophers: "The young deities discussed/ Laws of form, and metre just,/ Orb, quintessence, and sunbeams,/ What subsisteth and what seems." Seyd, the local informer, reports Uriel's treason to the "old war-gods." The heresy consists of Uriel's argument "against the being of a line." "Line in nature is not found," he says. "Unit and universe are round." At this the hero is banished and the gods throw a "forgetting wind" over the celestial beings whose lips thereafter hold the secret "If in ashes the fire-seed slept." But despite this, Uriel's truth remains a threat to the established order, for "truth-speaking things" occasionally substantiate Uriel's statements "And the gods shook, they knew not why." The political implications of this fable are clear: the truth will out and though Uriel has been banished he has planted the seed of rebellion. The theme is typically romantic in the sense that a self-reliant hero finds himself martyred by the authority of his society, yet manages somehow to subvert it.

If we look at the poem in esthetic terms, however, it becomes a useful demonstration of Emerson's essential problem, which was to translate his theory into a poetically meaningful accomplishment. Uriel's heresy consists in his argument for the organic principle which insists on the unity of nature. A line breaks at both ends and suggests something like the mechanism of Lockean and Newtonian systems. The circular image ("In vain produced, all rays return;/ Evil will bless, and ice will burn") is not merely the assertion of philosophical optimism, but seems a threat to the established order which apparently fears the suggestion that matter and spirit may be related. Emerson has given us something like a prelapsarian version of the fall, for the poem is set in Paradise before "the wild Time coined itself/ Into calendar months and days." Uriel is punished (like Adam) because he has gained possession of knowledge which only the older gods may have, and as in the Old Testament, the punishment is a veiling of direct knowledge, and "A sad self-knowledge" which "withering, fell/ On the beauty of Uriel." Uriel is forced to withdraw into his cloud and the secret of unity in nature is thenceforth withheld. This is similar to the argument I have discussed earlier in which Emerson defines the fall as a withdrawal of direct communion and its replacement by symbolism. Here Emerson develops the same point of view:

> But now and then, truth-speaking things
> Shamed the angels' veiling wings;

And, shrilling from the solar course,
Or from fruit of chemic force,
Procession of a soul in matter,
Or the speeding change of water,
Or out of the good of evil born,
Came Uriel's voice of cherub scorn,
And a blush tinged the upper sky,
And the gods shook, they knew not why.

The angels' veiling wings now seem to be keeping the secret from man as well as the celestial kind and Emerson has presented something like the Promethean myth, with Uriel in the latter's role. We can easily see, however, that "truth-speaking things" are the natural facts which no heavenly conspiracy can hide. The natural facts, indeed, constantly perform their function of revealing spiritual truths. But in presenting his argument, Emerson has neglected to implement his own theory of language. He has given us the spiritual truths but has not succeeded in wedding them to concrete representation of natural facts. Without this balance we have a philosophical statement barren of just those elements of language which Emerson had identified so well in his essays. The message is clear: despite the attempts by the gods to prevent us from knowing the truth about the organic unity of the universe, the very facts of nature provide man with a method of apprehending it. Natural facts, in short, are symbols of spiritual truths. What is missing from this formulation is the emphasis on symbolic language as one of the essential mediating elements in the process whereby the higher vision may be achieved. At the same time, Emerson's language is abstract and far removed from the level of diction he could occasionally inject into his essays, catching the excitement and force of vernacular speech. Natural facts are generalized under the term "truth-speaking things"; it takes some time to understand that it is rays of light which are "shrilling from the solar course," or precisely what is designated by "fruit of chemic force"; the meaning of "Procession of a soul in matter" clearly refers to the existence of man as a material and spiritual entity, but the expression does little to enforce the notion (we shall find a similar approach in Whitman's concern with the soul and the body); even the "speeding change of matter" (which must refer to the transformation of water, easily observed, into steam or ice) provides little sense of concreteness. The result is that nothing is clearly or carefully rendered or dramatized and the spiritual truths float about without any effective impact, and in obvious contradiction to Emerson's suggestions for a new kind of poetry. It will be instructive to keep Emerson's failure in mind when we look closely at Whitman's successful implementation of Emerson's epiphanic theory.

Emerson comes closer in a short poem, "Days," which has received a good deal of attention and which may be quoted in its entirety:

> Daughters of Time, the hypocritic Days,
> Muffled and dumb like barefoot dervishes,
> And marching single in an endless file,
> Bring diadems and fagots in their hands.
> To each they offer gifts after his will,
> Bread, kingdoms, stars, and sky that holds them all.
> I, in my pleached garden, watched the pomp,
> Forgot my morning wishes, hastily
> Took a few herbs and apples, and the Day
> Turned and departed silent. I, too late,
> Under her solemn fillet saw the scorn.

Here, though Emerson is still concerned with giving the moral (as D. H. Lawrence noted, in a passage to which I shall return, all art is moralistic but not didactic) it is carried by the metaphors and hence the innumerable connotations which he knew figurative language to contain are able to make themselves felt. F. O. Matthiessen has provided a valuable discussion of the poem in terms of its manifest and latent meaning. He relates it to the sense Emerson had of the polarities of life, especially the ebb and flow of artistic power. "He was ever being distracted," Matthiessen says, "by the disproportion between the means and the end, by the feeling that 'we are always getting ready to live, but never living.' There were so many years of education and earning a livelihood, of routine and sickness and travel, but 'very little life in a lifetime . . . a few, few hours in the longest.' In that state of mind all of existence seemed a disguise that he could not penetrate. Moreover, even when he was flooded with power, he had to confess to an inability to handle it."[12] The overt meaning then refers to his sense of guilt for not "penetrating . . . the disguise of appearance, for blindly neglecting to abandon himself at once to the mysteries of the Reason." The covert meaning, however, moves in a different direction: "His instinctive taking of the few herbs and apples is the fitting expression for his spontaneous trust in the amplitude to man's needs of his immediate surroundings. . . . His clinging to this frail harvest, even though he regrets it, is what empowers him here to suggest the poignant complexity of his existence. By means of his parable he has been true to both halves of his consciousness and has set going a dynamic tension between them."

We are always in Matthiessen's debt for his erudition and sensitivity to texts. But a close reading of the poem in the light of Emerson's esthetic both amplifies Matthiessen's views and quarrels with them. The theme of the poem may also be related to the problem of choice and if we put it in this framework some of the images come into focus. The days are seen as female, daughters of father time and hence by definition, hypocritic. The sources of this view are rather traditional and lean heavily on the implied meaning of the Old Testament story of the fall, in which the woman through duplicity seduces man to his downfall. Emerson's scene is set in a garden—in New England, to be sure; but the oriental images suggest strongly a double focus which brings together the New World and the Old. If this is a parable, as Matthiessen suggests, it is a more familiar one than he has suspected. And we may then suggest that the statement cf the theme caⅡ be enlarged to include not only the problem of choice, but the results which follow upon it. Hence we need to note an irony in the line, "To each they offer gifts after his will," for the hypocrisy of the daughters consists in their foreknowledge of what will come to pass. Emerson indeed has given us a variation of the myth of the fall, and like his Puritan forefathers he is aware that its truth is justified not merely by its statement in the Old Testament, but by the fact of its recurrence in every generation. (Perry Miller has repeatedly shown in his invaluable studies of American Puritanism that its major appeal has always been to the brute facts of man's experience.) We do not need an authority to remind us that each man reproduces the original sin in his own terms and thus reveals the legitimacy of his punishment. As Michael Wigglesworth put it, in the words that Christ speaks to the children who have not yet had the opportunity to sin in their lives, yet find themselves being judged to damnation:

> You think If we had been as he,
>   whom God did so betrust,
> We to our cost would ne'er have lost
>   all for a paltry lust.
> Had you been made in Adam's stead,
>   you would like things have wrought,
> And so into the self-same woe,
>   yourselves and yours have brought.

The days seem to offer man a free choice after his own will, but man is by his nature bound to choose incorrectly, and indeed there is some reason to believe that the poem suggests a degree of predestination. (That is, in any case, a knotty theological problem which we need not concern ourselves with here. A degree of predestination is not far from saying a little bit pregnant.) Nevertheless, the narrator of the poem, reproduces the fatal act; significantly he takes the herb and apple (I am not sure if herb carries a connotation similar to apple in the myth, suggesting as it does both noxious and medicinal qualities) from the woman and discovers, too late, the irreversible condition of his destiny. The final statement of the theme, then, leads us to an awareness of man's fate. Only too late is he made aware of the limitations of the human condition. As the day itself is inexorably lengthened, so is he bound to forget his "morning wishes" (which suggest both innocence and youth) and fall victim to the unconquerable flow of time. The Father, though absent, asserts His overwhelming power, and forces man to become aware of his weakness and humility.

I find it difficult, then, to follow, the second of Matthiessen's readings. Emerson clearly gives us a sense of the complexity of man's condition, but in a very conventional statement derived from Judaeo-Christian tradition, which should not surprise us when it comes from a minister whose connection with Puritanism extends to several generations. It is true, however, that if we read herbs and apples as natural facts, then the choice was appropriate in terms of Emerson's esthetic. Yet the Days clearly scorn it, and while the narrator may be seen to be in the dark, the daughters of time can hardly be wrong. The issue is best understood in the framework of Emerson's handling of the materialism-idealism issue. In this sense, the suggested correct choice ("stars and sky that holds them all") is equally fallible, for it fails to take into account the necessary movement through the material in order to attain the spiritual truth. Here it seems to me the consistency of Emerson's application of his theory fails, as it so often does in his poetry. For the seemingly correct choice which would have earned him the approbation of the Days is sheer Platonism—the mistake he strongly criticizes organized religion for making.

Yet we need to agree with Matthiessen's estimate of the effectiveness of the poem, though on other grounds. Its strength comes partly from the darker (hence less simpleminded view) of existence which it suggests. Indeed Emerson's esthetic works in both directions, as Melville's work reveals. Emerson had insisted that there "is no object so foul that intense light will not make beautiful." If one carefully chooses the natural facts to include essentially only those rosy elements of life, the spiritual truths which follow will always substantiate Emerson's contention. (On some occasions, however, the impact of the natural fact will make itself felt despite the attempt to absorb it in a pleasant vision; an example is Emerson's discussion of circumcision, which he uses to illustrate his dictum that the "vocabulary of an omniscient man would embrace words and images excluded from polite conversation. . . . The circumcision is an example of the power of poetry to raise the low and offensive. Small and mean things serve as well as great symbols. [It seems clear that Emerson missed the humor of this juxtaposition.] The meaner the type by which a law is expressed, the more pungent it is, and the more lasting in the memories of men." (Whitman obviously learned this lesson well.) But Melville, using an esthetic similar to Emerson's, simply reversed his view and pointed out that there is no object so beautiful that intense light will not reveal the underlying horror. Moreover, given the natural facts which Melville identifies (the sea, sharks, the great whale itself), his position is as easily justified. Emerson could rarely bring himself to this view, but in "Days" he departs from his usual optimism.

But the poem does substantiate another element in Emerson's characteristic argument for symbolic language. His reliance on metaphor and a very commonplace diction does indeed release the mythic underpinnings which he insisted language contained. If we recall "Uriel" it is notable that his conscious use of myth and allusion simply does not come off. Emerson's own analysis helps us to see why: the allusions to Uriel (an archangel of the sun who appears in the Old Testament and in Milton as well) are applied from the surface and function as ornament rather than as organic expressions of the content. The influence of Milton in this respect was bound to be destructive to Emerson's powers, as he should have been the first to see, and that may explain as well his reliance on just those techniques of generalization in language which his theories helped Whitman to avoid. In "Days" Emerson was not only on his own ground, he was able to provide a proof of his notions that even the most commonplace subject could release the greatest spiritual force. Unlike Whitman, he could not develop his ideas fully in his poetry, but there is no avoiding the fact that the ideological implications of the poem expose a failure of nerve (or metaphor) in Emerson's inability or unwillingness to place the deserving value on the natural fact. Still, as Matthiessen again informs us, Emerson thought "Days" his best poem and we can agree that it came closest to enforcing his esthetic philosophy.

Emerson's theories were effectively utilized by Whitman, whose poems show directly the impact of Emerson's esthetic. Equally concerned with folk ideology, Whitman was possessed of a poetic talent that far outstripped Emerson's muse. His poem, "Song of Myself," with its Emersonian epiphanies, "loose fingered chords," and catalogues of natural facts, shows more clearly how Emerson's esthetic provided a means of using folk tradition in the context of a sophisticated literary theory.

Chapter Three
The Emerson-Whitman Tradition: Whitman

HERDER'S HOPES for the growth of "new blossoms" in America when the Old World became decadent was one of numerous conceptions which identified the United States as the site of a new Garden of Eden. And it is significant that he should have expressed the idea that became the leading motif in Whitman's thought, even to the use of a metaphor like that chosen by Whitman for the title of his major work. Whitman's leaves of grass sprang from American soil, but as I shall show here much of his characteristic thought was distinctly Herderian. As in the case of Emerson the question of Herder's impact is involved in much more than tracing influences. Herder's ideas about nationalism, poetry, and folk art were available to many thinkers and writers; if they found in Whitman incredibly fertile soil, it was to a great extent because he was already thinking along similar lines. At the same time, Whitman's extremist tendencies led him to push Herder's theories even further than Emerson, and, like the latter, Whitman drew some inferences from Herder that his European followers overlooked.

All the sources of Herder's ideas in nineteenth-century America were available to Whitman. As Pochmann observes: "It is not necessary to speculate on whether Whitman read Herder in translation or relied on criticism and commentary. He had access to both, in books and periodicals, American as well as British."[1] A good many of Herder's views were transmitted by Emerson to the impressionable Whitman, who admitted, "I was simmering, simmering, simmering; Emerson brought me to a boil." But placing Whitman in this framework will help us to understand a major problem which none of his serious critics has been able to evade—the annoying question of the nationalistic fervor which pervades much of the poet's work. Unfriendly as well as friendly critics, in fact, find it possible to denigrate much of Whitman's poetry and prose by emphasizing what they identify as the essential provincialism or chauvinism of his thought.[2] And since almost everyone who has written about him agrees that, good or bad, Whitman is the aboriginal American poet, it has been a simple matter to explain his ethnocentrism as an outgrowth of the American experience. It is not surprising, therefore, that in the running debate over whether or not an American literature exists, Whitman is usually one of the central figures. But even those writers who find Whitman's point of view congenial have so far failed to delineate the respects in which he may be distinguished from truly jingoistic or provincial poets. For it seems to me useless as well as misleading to deny that chauvinism has been (and is) deeply rooted in many phases of American thought. It is true that the American brand of nationalism has been weighted quite out of proportion to its European counterparts—Chauvin, after all, was a Frenchman and even the most extreme American nationalists have been pretty tame when they are compared with the variety of chauvinists who overran Germany, Italy, Japan, and the Soviet Union in our own time. Another approach has justified American nationalism by recalling the persistent arguments by native as well as foreign critics that America is, in fact, not a distinct nation but simply a pale reflection of the Europe from which most of its people are descended. But none of the arguments can really efface from our memories the brutality and inhumanity which have often resulted from what appeared to be simply the affirmation of national aspirations.

While it is easy for some to represent Whitman as nothing but a craven chauvinist (by quoting individual lines from his poetry and prose) the core of his thought and his literary theory are informed by a full commitment to humanistic rather than narrowly nationalistic ideals. My contention is that Whitman's humanistic nationalism can best be understood by examining what I shall call his folkloristic arguments for an American literature; moreover, I submit that although he reworked them to fit American conditions, Whitman's program for the establishing of a national literature followed closely the conceptions of Herder. It was within this ideological framework that Whitman implemented Emerson's esthetic formulations.

That he was fully aware of Herder's key conceptions is indicated in the comment with which Whitman ended *A Backward Glance O'er Travell'd Roads*: "Concluding with two items for the imaginative genius of the West, when it worthily rises—First, what Herder taught to the young Goethe, that really great poetry is always (like the Homeric or Biblical canticles) the result of a national spirit, and not the privilege of a polish'd and select few; Second, that the strongest and sweetest songs yet remain to be sung."[3] Thus it was to Whitman's sense of the national roots of literature that Herder's notions had their greatest appeal. The persistent denials of American cultural independence, however, had prompted Whitman to write in 1847 when he was editor of the Brooklyn *Daily Eagle*: "*Are* we not a 'mere suburb of London'? We trow yes . . . as long as we copy with servile imitation, the very cast-off literary fashions of London—as long as we wait for English critics to stamp our books and our authors, before *we* presume to say they are very good or very bad—as long as the floods of British manufactured books are poured over the land, and give their color to all the departments of taste and opinion. . . . The 'United States an independent country'? Why we are politically independent no doubt; but the United States are as much bound in mental bondage as ever—as much as Gulliver was bound by the Lilliputians."[4] This image of America as a giant in chains persisted in Whitman's thought, though even in his early discussions he was full of optimism for America's prospects. One source of this optimism was his belief "that God has given the American mind powers of analysis and acuteness superior to those possessed by any other nation on earth." The remedy, therefore, to the state of American dependence on Europe, Whitman explained, is obvious. "Let those who read, —(and in this country who does not read?)—no more condescend to patronize an inferior author, when they have so many respectable writers at home. Shall Hawthorne get a paltry *seventy-five dollars* for a two-volume work?—Shall real American genius shiver with neglect while the public run after this foreign trash? We hope, and we confidently expect, that the people of this land will come to their 'sober second thought' upon the subject, and that soon." If Whitman's argument seems blatantly chauvinistic, it was the result of his deep revulsion against the widespread attitude that America was infantile, barbaric, and hence devoid of any native literary culture. Even in this early period, however, he was careful to distinguish between "Petty bigotted nationality" and the encouragement of native authors. "For the beautiful creations of the great intellects of Europe," he wrote, "we of the Western World bring our tribute of admiration and respect."

It was precisely in his attempt to provide proof of the vigor and dignity of American materials that Whitman profited most from Herder's formulations. He took more literally even than Emerson Herder's proposal that national literary culture should be based on the creations of the folk. Grafting this point of view to his fiercely democratic ideology, Whitman constructed a defense of the creative power of the common people that represented a unique adaptation of Herder's position to the conditions of American society. Herder had argued that recognizing the value inherent in folk art might bring into existence a truly humanitarian, democratic culture. Whitman began with the assumption of political democracy and then emphasized the irony of America's dependence on the aristocratic literary culture of Europe. Even Emerson, who had argued forcefully for the recognition of a democratic literature, was too genteel for Whitman's taste. "For a philosopher," Whitman reflected in later years, "Emerson possessed a singularly dandified theory of manners." Whitman implied that Emerson's New England background and his "cold and bloodless intellectuality" prevented him from participating fully in the democratic ferment which Whitman perceived taking place in America. The establishing of a democratic culture had little to do with manners and was, according to Whitman, quite distinct from anything that had ever existed in history before: "The plan of a select class, superfined, (demarcated from the rest), the plan of Old World lands and literatures, is not so objectionable in itself, but because it chokes the true plan for us, and indeed is death to it. As to such special class, the United States can never produce any equal to the splendid show (far, far, beyond comparison or competition here) of the principal European nations, both in the past and at the present day. But an immense and distinctive commonalty over our vast and varied area, west and east, south and north—in fact, for the first time in history, a great aggregated real PEOPLE, worthy the name, and made of develop'd heroic individuals, both sexes—is America's principal, perhaps only, reason for being." The passage reveals Whitman's leading motif, what he called "the most profound theme that can occupy the mind of man"—the representation in poetry of "the (radical, democratic) Me . . . on the one side," and the "(conservative) Not Me . . . on the other." In fact his poetry is essentially an argument for the organic unity of the individual with mankind and all of nature. The agent who reveals this relationship is the bard and his vehicle is poetry. But the success of the whole plan depends on the notion that the highest poetic values reside with the folk rather than with established, formal traditions.

Whitman extended the democratic elements in Herder's theory until the bard became a democratic prophet: "The prophet and the bard/ Shall yet maintain themselves, in higher stages yet,/ Shall mediate to the Modern, to Democracy," he wrote. As in earlier epochs, Whitman insisted, the poet would be one with his people, symbolizing in his own person the aspirations of all: "The American bards shall be mark'd for generosity and affection, and for encouraging competitors. They shall be Kosmos, without monopoly or secrecy, glad to pass anything to anyone—hungry for equals night and day. They shall not be careful of riches and privilege—they shall be riches and privilege—they shall perceive who the most affluent man is. The most affluent man is he that confronts all the shows he sees by equivalents out of the stronger wealth of himself. The American bard shall delineate no class of persons, nor one or two out of the strata of interests, nor love most nor truth most, nor the soul most, nor the body most —and not be for the Eastern states more than the Western, or the Northern states more than the Southern." This was Whitman's re-statement of the familiar notion that the bard, in ancient times, was the spokesman for his communal group. But if the bard was to be, in Emerson's terms, a "representative man," then it was necessary for Whitman to demonstrate that underlying the vastness and diversity of America there was indeed some basis for unity. When he is echoing Emerson, Whitman identifies this coherence as Nature, which is unchanging and eternal, leading always to the world of spirit. More often, however, Whitman's attitude is historical rather than metaphysical; he defines the basis for communal coherence in terms of the unique history of the United States. Americans, he argues, are literally a new creation in a New World and can justly claim that they have evolved a freshly-made cosmos. The American bard is not an anachronism, a throwback to the races of primitive man in antiquity: "(As if it were necessary to trot back generation after generation to the Eastern records! As if the beauty and sacredness of the demonstrable must fall behind that of the mythical! As if the opening of the western continent by discovery and what has transpired since in North and South America were less than the small theatre of the antique or the aimless sleepwalking of the middle ages.)" But because the inhabitants of this continent are a new and young community, they are unranked in the hierarchy of cultures and represent, in the eyes of the "civilized" world, a savage and barbaric people.

The identification of the American as a "new Adam" and of America as a "virgin land" has been shown, by R. W. B. Lewis and Henry Nash Smith, to have deep roots in European as well as in American thought. Lewis, in *The American Adam,* has shown that Whitman habitually writes as if there were no historical past outside America —even outside his own individual experience. And Smith, in *Virgin Land,* has exposed the ambivalence which resulted from the American's attempt to espouse a primal innocence as well as the idea of historical progress. But Whitman's connection with Herder led him to suggest another conclusion which could be drawn from the peculiarities of the American experience. For Whitman, the designation of America as essentially barbaric became advantageous, since it enabled him to capitalize upon Herder's view that primitive communities contain the energy and creative force upon which a national literature must be based. It is important to recall that Herder's conception is not a celebration of primitivism for its own sake; folklore is the well from which formal literature is drawn. And here, Whitman argued, was not merely a small isolated *Volk* from which a national literature might be eveloved; rather, America contained an entire population in that state of "barbarism" from which, folklorists had insisted, the germinating power of folk art was derived. It was to a great extent from the contemplation of this prospect that Whitman's enthusiasm and audacity were generated. Indeed, he sounded his "barbaric yawp over the roofs of the world" to celebrate his knowledge of the power he had discovered.

Whitman's intellectual commitment to the idea of progress, moreover, was a further check against antiquarianism or outright primitivism. His view of the effort by Americans to create a completely democratic state was expressed in a "transcendental metaphysic which made reform and democracy the goals of cosmic history."[5] America represented a recreation, on a higher level, of a vital, rough culture akin to those of ancient times, but different by virtue of its conscious affirmation of equalitarianism. The role of the democratic bard, consequently, changed in response to the new conditions. The Romantic bard (as he was seen by eighteenth- and nineteenth-century writers) resided serenely among the wilds of nature. The democratic bard, who often flourished in the cities, was more like the Hebrew prophet, who excoriated a stiff-necked people. Whitman does indeed explode with the force of an Isaiah or Micah. "By this writer," he proclaimed in his own anonymous and highly favorable review of *Leaves of Grass,* "the rules of polite circles are dismissed with scorn. Your stale modesties, he seems to say, are filthy to such a man as I."[6] And in the letter addressed to Emerson which Whitman appended to the second edition of his book, he posed the same question which Herder and Emerson asked of their contemporaries: "Where are any mental expressions from you beyond what you have copied or stolen? Where are the born throngs of poets, literats, orators, you promised? Will you but tag after other nations? . . . You are young, have the perfectest of dialects, a free press, a free government, the world forwarding its best to be with you. As justice has been strictly done to you, from this hour do strict justice to yourself. . . . Submit to the most robust bard till he remedy your barrenness. Then you will not need to adopt the heirs of others; you will have true heirs, begotten of yourself, blooded with your own blood." As Herder had noted, the injection of folk art into the veins of sophisticated literary culture would result in a cleansing and revitalizing of literature. One of Whitman's favorite metaphors is based on just this notion: ". . . the sane, eternal moral and spiritual esthetic attributes . . . will gradually enter into the chyle of sociology and literature. They will finally make the blood and brawn of the best individualities of both sexes . . . dominate the new World."

The ultimate source of such vitality, Whitman understood, was language and he drew significant inferences from the work of folklorists and philologists. In "Slang in America" he wrote: "Language, be it remembered, is not an abstract construction of the learn'd, or of dictionary makers, but it is something arising out of the work, needs, ties, joys, affections, tastes, of long generations of humanity, and has its bases broad and low, close to the ground. Its final decisions are made by the masses, people nearest the concrete, having most to do with actual land and sea. It impermeates all, the Past as well as the Present, and is the grandest triumph of the human intellect." He gave credit to the "honest delvings, as of late years, by the German and British workers in comparative philology," viewing their discoveries not only as a glimpse into the past, but also as a guide for the present. Here was additional confirmation of Whitman's belief that the wells of artistic power sprang from the common people. And just as Homer, Ossian, and the biblical bards had created their poetry out of the language of the people, so the modern bard must find his inspiration and materials in the language and diction of the common people of his own culture. Slang is "the lawless germinal element, below all words and sentences, and behind all poetry, and proves a certain perennial rankness and protestantism in speech. As the United States inherit by far their most precious possession—the language they talk and write—from the Old World, under and out of its feudal institutes, I will allow myself to borrow a simile even of those forms farthest removed from American democracy. Considering Language then as some mighty potentate, into the majestic audience-hall of the monarch ever enters a personage like one of Shakespeare's clowns, and takes position there, and plays a part even in the stateliest ceremonies. Such is Slang, or indirection, an attempt of common humanity to escape from bald literalism, and express itself illimitably, which in prehistoric times gave the start to, and perfected, the whole immense tangle of the old mythology." Slang undermines conventional literature, as the religious dissenters subverted the established church; like the clowns in Shakespeare, it performs a crucial role despite its low status. Although folklorists and philologists tended to limit their analyses of the poetry-making ability of the folk to primitive societies, Whitman makes a point of having discovered the same processes at work in the cities of America: "I find the same rule in the people's conversations everywhere. I heard this among the men of the city horse-cars, where the conductor is often call'd a 'snatcher'. . . . In the slang of New York common restaurant waiters a plate of ham and beans is known as 'stars and stripes,' codfish balls as 'sleeve buttons,' and hash as 'mystery.' " This is what later folklorists came to call the "folk process," and Whitman was not shocked by its impertinences. Indeed he used similar approaches in his own poetry.

It is not surprising that he should note precisely those areas of American life which would ultimately produce the materials for a new canon of American folksong. "Certainly," he observed, "philologists have not given enough attention to this slang element and its results, which I repeat, can probably be found working everywhere today, amid modern conditions, with as much life and activity as in far-back Greece or India under prehistoric ones. Then the wit—the rich flashes of humor and genius and poetry—darting out often from a gang of laborers, railroad-men, miners, drivers, or boatmen! How often have I hovered at the edge of a crowd of them to hear their repartees and impromptus! You get more real fun from half an hour with them than from the books of all the 'American humorists.' " It was not until the next century (and largely through the work of John and Alan Lomax) that the work songs and occupational songs of America would figure prominently in the identification of an American folksong tradition.

It is noteworthy that, except for a few early pieces on patriotic themes, Whitman wrote no literary ballads. He boasted of his emancipation from what he called the "ballad style" of poetry, meaning a form dependent on meter and rhyme. For the English and German romantic poets as well as nineteenth-century American writers, the literary ballad seemed to be the form which most closely approximated folk poetry. Whitman was unique in his resistance to the mere copying of forms derived from ballads which, he noted, were essentially based on legends concerning kings and aristocracy, and thus not fit for the poet of democracy. Hence critics have often commented on the lack of folk influence in Whitman's poetry. But it is more accurate to note that Whitman rejected the surface forms in favor of major philosophical principles and approaches based on folk tradition. At the same time Whitman revealed how well he had understood Emerson's conception of self-reliance. "The best part of Emersonianism is," Whitman wrote in 1882, "it breeds the giant that destroys itself." But as in Emerson it was a sense of individualism that took serious account of the communal resources of the artist. Slang thus provided Whitman with a metaphor that united perfectly his political and esthetic vision. It prefigured from the beginning the ultimate political as well as esthetic triumph of the commonalty, the "en-masse." It is the poet who inherits the language of his people, but he must raise it to the highest levels in his own terms. For this reason the approach of both Emerson and Whitman represented an extremely fertile resource for twentieth-century American artists and writers who were interested in identifying the roots of native culture. Joseph J. Kwiat has pointed out, for example, the influence of the Emerson-Whitman tradition on the American painter, Robert Henri: "Emerson's doctrine of self-reliance and his profound respect for the dignity of the individual particularly impressed and influenced Henri. These Emersonian theories gave an impetus to Henri's already critical attitude toward the smug, hypocritical, and provincial cultural state of his native country. They also initiated his driving desire for a vital and individual conception of art which would contribute toward the emancipation of American culture from the enervating grasp of the Academy and the Genteel Tradition. For the mature Henri, however, Walt Whitman was even more influential than Emerson in strengthening his appreciation and understanding of individuality. Whitman's special significance as a 'force for freedom' is evident in Henri's parallel views on many problems—artistic, social, political, and cultural."[7]

Viewed from the perspective of Herder's folk ideology, Whitman's nationalism shows itself to be far removed from a petty chauvinism. What Herder taught to the young Goethe, Whitman found instructive for his own attempt to uncover the roots of an American literature. But just as folksong signified to Herder a principle of equality in his history of civilization, so Whitman's celebration of the "divine average" transcended the limits of American experience. In fact, Whitman's attitude toward the value of folk art (best expressed in his affirmation of a vernacular diction for American poetry) provides a clue to the vision of brotherhood explicit in his poetry and prose. For it is interesting to note that while critics have found Whitman's nationalistic fervor troublesome, they have had similar difficulties explaining the internationalism in his thought. Malcolm Cowley, for example, has concluded that Whitman's work is "full of separate statements and hints and intuitions . . . that are dangerous as philosophical guides because they point in all directions."[8] The first pair in a list of what Cowley calls "quarreling tendencies" is Nationalism and Internationalism. Discounting these inconsistencies as misleading, Cowley finds the source of Whitman's affirmation of brotherhood to be homosexualism, or loneliness, which led him to a sense of "brotherhood or identity with all the outcasts and diseased and rejected of the earth," just as other critics have traced it to Quakerism or the influence of Emerson.

And perhaps all of these may very well have counted in making Whitman what he finally came to be.

But there seems every justification to argue that Whitman found a major source for his notion of human brotherhood in Herder's view that national culture, by virtue of its being rooted in folk tradition, is a stage in the development of an international and universal culture. The idea received a new impetus in Whitman's thought because it was grafted on to a frankly democratic ideology which, at least in theory, was already committed to the notion that America's unique destiny was to fulfill the age-old prophecy of equalitarianism. The barbaric yawp, ironically, was to announce that the nation least respected by the "aristocracies" and civilized countries of the Old World had brought into being a society fully capable of implementing the dream of world brotherhood. The art of the folk (in song or in a vernacular diction) is the means whereby a national literature may be created; but it is also a forecast of the final stage, the "passage to more than India." As Whitman himself put it: "Lately, I have wondered whether the last meaning of this cluster of thirty-eight states is not only practical fraternity among themselves . . . but for fraternity over the whole globe—that dazzling, pensive dream of ages! Indeed, the peculiar glory of our lands, I have come to see, or expect to see, not in their geographical or republican greatness, nor wealth or products, nor military or naval power . . . , but more and more in a vaster, saner, more surrounding Comradeship, uniting closer and closer not only the American States, but all nations, and all humanity."[9] That vision is framed in terms very much like the deepest intimations of Herder's conception of the "equal validity of incommensurable cultures."

Whitman is no simple, folk poet, nor did he ever attempt to be. Yet it is worth looking at his work in terms of the folk ideology he adapted from both Herder and Emerson, and especially in the context of the latter's esthetic. All these counted heavily in his development and will help us to understand why Whitman stands at the center of our poetic tradition and the folkloristic movements closely related to it. To begin with, we can place in a more accurate context Whitman's conscious attempts to create in such a poem as "Song of Myself" a national expression akin to epic. But we can see at once that mere imitation of traditional epic forms would have been unthinkable for him. That would be merely another variation of the reliance on European influences that Whitman and Emerson so furiously opposed in

the literary productions of many of their contemporaries. (It is worth recalling that Longfellow's American "epic," *Song of Hiawatha*, which leaned heavily on the matter and, unfortunately, the meter of the Finnish *Kalevala*, was published in 1855.) Yet in the preface to the first edition of *Leaves of Grass*, Whitman makes clear the national character of his effort: "America does not repel the past or what it has produced under its forms or amid other politics or the idea of castes or the old religions . . . accepts the lesson with calmness . . . is not so impatient as has been supposed that the slough still sticks to opinions and manners and literature while the life which served its requirements has passed into the new life of the new forms . . . perceives that the corpse is slowly borne from the eating and sleeping rooms of the house . . . perceives that it waits a little while in the door . . . that it was fittest for its days . . . that its action has descended to the stalwart and wellshaped heir who approaches . . . and that he shall be fittest for his days." This is not a doctrine of the survival of the fittest, but an acknowledgement that every age has its own appropriate expression and that each must be taken for its own worth. The heirs will benefit from what has passed but will express their own integrity and for Whitman the difference is easy to see: "Other states indicate themselves in their deputies . . . but the genius of the United States is not best or most in its executives or legislatures, nor in its ambassadors or authors or colleges or churches or parlors, nor even in its newspapers or inventors . . . but always most in the common people. Their manner, speech, dress, friendships—the freshness and candor of their physiognomy—the picturesque looseness of their carriage . . . their deathless attachment to freedom—their aversion to anything indecorous or soft or mean—the practical acknowledgement of the citizens of one state by the citizens of all other states—the fierceness of their roused resentment—their curiosity and welcome of novelty—their self-esteem and wonderful sympathy— their susceptibility to a sleight—the air they have of persons who never knew how it felt to stand in the presence of superiors—the fluency of their speech—their delight in music, the sure symptom of manly tenderness and native elegance of soul . . . their good temper and openhandedness—the terrible significance of their elections—the President's taking off his hat to them not they to him—these too are unrhymed poetry. It awaits the gigantic and generous treatment worthy of it." The major irony of the title is evident from this list of Whitman's concerns, for the "Song of Myself" is a tribute to the spirit of a people, an attempt, as Whitman indicates, to delineate the manners,

the temper, and the very gestures of the common man. In that sense Whitman may be related to epic, as we understand it to be the song of a nation.

But the idea of epic will not take us very far. The great application that Whitman made of the organic principle was to insist that, as Emerson had already argued, the content was primary and the form will flow naturally from it if the poet opens himself to the influences of his nation and the resources of his consciousness. As Whitman conceived himself a new Adam in a New World, so his poetry had to be a new utterance in a radically different form. The main criticism of Whitman is still based on his sense of novelty which is seen as the major cause of his poetic failings. To put it another way, Whitman remains the great barbarian who, in the process of creating his own savage world, has succeeded only in losing the advantages of civilization. But other elements in his work have suggested that there was something remarkably sophisticated, even avant-garde, in his literary productions; and critics have tended to identify this as a paradox. If Whitman is a barbarian, how can we explain his association with the Symbolists and Joyce? Why does his best work have so contemporary a sound? Richard Chase, who has provided what I find to be the most perceptive reading of Whitman, nevertheless finds him "paradoxically extremely civilized and extremely primitive. Both semanticist and bard, he is a kind of primitive I. A. Richards and a sophisticated Orpheus. As a poet who wishes to create a mythic poetry he is confronted with the dilemma (the democratic dilemma, Tocqueville would say) of a sensibility which quickens to mythic feeling only at opposite ends of the spectrum, either in spontaneous, inchoate, 'germinal' experience or in abstractions such as Mother, Father, Equality, Love, or Democracy. What he lacks, as compared with Homer, for example, or Dante or Milton, is a mediating body of mythic narrative and metaphor."[10] This is the familiar argument which has been made for the difficulties of most of our nineteenth-century writers who, like Hawthorne, bewail the lack of a feudal past to provide the sources of literature. It is an argument which I shall return to later on, for we find it again in the context of folklore research. It calls to mind Hawthorne's comment in the introduction to *The Scarlet Letter* where he apologizes for having muffed the opportunities to create a novel based on the teeming and colorful life that abounded in the environs of the Custom House: "The fault was mine. The page of life that was spread out before me seemed dull and commonplace only because I had not fathomed its deeper import. A better book than I shall ever write was there; leaf after leaf presenting itself to me, just as it was written."

Instead, he confessed, his "eyes fastened themselves upon the old scarlet letter, and would not be turned aside. Certainly, there was some deep meaning in it, most worthy of interpretation, and which, as it were, streamed forth from the mystic symbol, subtly communicating itself to my sensibilities, but evading the analysis of my mind." Lacking the continuity of a prose tradition such as existed in the English novel, Hawthorne was forced back on his own devices. What he discovered was a mythopoeic tradition which he called "romance," distinguishing it from the realism of European prose writing. Sitting in the deserted parlor of his home in front of the coal fire, Hawthorne hoped to find a source of inspiration for his writing the next day: "If the imaginative faculty refused to act at such an hour, it might well be deemed a hopeless case. Moonlight, in a familiar room, falling so white upon the carpet, and showing all its figures so distinctly,—making every object so minutely visible, yet so unlike a morning or noontide visibility,—is a medium the most suitable for a romance writer to get acquainted with his illusive guests. There is the little domestic scenery of the well-known apartment; the chairs, with each its separate individuality; the centre-table, sustaining a work basket, a volume or two, and an extinguished lamp; the sofa; the book-case; the picture on the wall—all these details, so completely seen, are so spiritualized by the unusual light, that they seem to lose their actual substance, and become things of intellect. Nothing is too small or too trifling to undergo this change, and acquire dignity thereby. A child's shoe; the doll, seated in her little wicker carriage; the hobby-horse;—whatever, in a word has been used or played with, during the day, is now invested with a quality of strangeness and remoteness, though still almost as vividly present as by daylight. Thus, therefore, the floor of our familiar room has become a neutral territory, somewhere between the real world and fairy-land, where the Actual and the Imaginary may meet, and each imbue itself with the nature of the other." This is, in a sense, an archetypal statement of the experience of our writers in the nineteenth century and later, and it has been accurately defined as what happens when the writer has no literary past to lean upon. But we have already encountered it before in Emerson's "transparent eyeball" passage. The elements are startlingly alike. It is an attempt to create an epiphany by working through the natural facts to reveal the underlying spiritual truths. "Nothing is too small or too trifling to undergo this change," Hawthorne asserts and it recalls Emerson's comment, "The invariable mark of wisdom is to see the miraculous in the common." Similarly, Hawthorne gives us a catalogue of natural facts which will help to provide the same sense of concreteness at the bottom of a mystical expression that Emerson found essential in his formulation. There is clearly a symbolist mode operating here, but as in Emerson, Hawthorne will not allow the form to overwhelm the content. If it could be accomplished, the epiphany would reveal a "neutral territory" where the "Actual and the Imaginary" may come together, each to infuse the other with its characteristics.

There is nothing shocking in this example of Hawthorne's utilizing a technique which seems precisely Emersonian in its essential formulations. He knew well enough not only Emerson but the whole range of Transcendentalist thinkers from Thoreau to Alcott. And given the possibilities of language, he could easily have come to a similar theory quite on his own. But I think it worth emphasizing that Hawthorne's critics are content to acknowledge his accomplishments despite their admission that democratic societies could provide no nourishment for art. And perhaps it is because Hawthorne agrees with the dictum, as his persistent apologies reveal. Yet I think we are wrong to take his statements at face value. Precisely because the Americans were out of the mainstream of European literary tradition they were able to create a literature of their own which, far from being provincial, as they humbly confessed, was in fact in the forefront by a hundred years of the kind of esthetic much valued by critics and writers in our own time. Emerson had already provided the esthetic as well as the insights which explain how this could occur, and a key perception was his awareness that "as we go back in history, language becomes more picturesque, until its infancy, when it is all poetry; or all spiritual facts are represented by natural symbols. . . . And as this is the first language, so is it the last." Northrop Frye has made a similar comment upon the reappearance of myth motifs in literature. It is not, he points out, that myth appears early in literature and then somehow is picked up at later moments by writers. Myth is at the center of language and is theoretically always a possible mode of expression. The same is true of symbolism. But as we have seen, Emerson understood that conventional and established literary traditions tend to cut off this ubiquitous source and substitute for it the comfortable formulas which satisfy their own accepted views.

Part of the response to Hawthorne, however, comes from the approbation of his craftsmanship as well as his awareness of the limitations in the human condition. We rarely talk about his primitivism or find him paradoxical. Whitman, on the other hand, is so full of bravado and tall talk that most of his critics find him shallow (at crucial moments) and unaware of what he was doing, or simply wrong in his major assumptions. Yet I think that Whitman was essentially more accurate than Hawthorne in his awareness of the nature of his position as an American poet and correct in not apologizing for it. The combination of his awareness of the powers of language (politically as well as symbolically) and his recognition of the potentialities of Emerson's esthetic were enough and Whitman knew it. There is, in short, no paradox in Whitman's sophisticated insights into the nature of symbolism and his acclamation of the folk sources of poetic power, which provided just such a body of "mediating mythic narrative" as Chase calls for.

I think we can see this best by looking closely at "Song of Myself" as a manifestation of Emerson's esthetic, for it will also help us to suggest answers to several other questions which have remained problematical in Whitman scholarship. The major one which has tantalized Whitman's critics is the question of the poem's form. The preface provides innumerable clues. The "expression of the American poet is to be transcendent and new. It is to be indirect and not direct or descriptive or epic. Its quality goes through these to much more. Let the age and wars of other nations be chanted and their eras and characters be illustrated and that finish the verse. Not so the great psalm of the republic. Here comes one among the well beloved stonecutters and plans with decision and science and sees the solid and beautiful forms of the future where there are now no solid forms." F. O. Matthiessen has shown that the term "indirection" in Whitman refers back to Emerson's idea of symbolism and indeed to Emerson's esthetic in general. But Matthiessen is disturbed by what he identifies as "one of the most confusing aspects of Whitman, the easy-hearted way he could shuttle back and forth from materialism to idealism without troubling himself about any inconsistency."[11] He is at his best, Matthiessen notes, when he insists that "imagination and actuality" need to be joined—and we might observe how close this is to Hawthorne's formulation. But I find it difficult to follow Matthiessen when he adds that "in spite of his enthusiasm for the natural sciences as well as for every other manifestation of progress, he never came very close to a scientific realism." I think this reveals Matthiessen's Marxist bias which seems uncomfortable in the presence of idealism. But we will be on safer grounds if we recall Emerson's approach to the relationship between materialism and idealism, in which the former is the essential channel for arriving at spiritual truths. Whitman's aim was not scientific realism, but the evocation of those delicious awakenings that Emerson described, and like the latter he recognized that the epiphany could only be achieved through a conscious manipulation of language in the context of natural facts. His search for "solid and beautiful forms" led him to note that "folks expect of the poet to indicate more than the beauty and dignity which always attach to dumb real objects . . . they expect him to indicate the path between reality and their souls." When the "facts are showered over with light," the poet's language will release its power and show itself to be the "medium that shall well nigh express the inexpressible." But if, as Whitman suggested, his poems were "only a language experiment," it was carried out in the context of an attitude toward language as "the dialect of common sense," a "powerful language of resistance" enlisted in the attempt to "breed one goodshaped and wellhung man, and a woman to be his perfect and independent mate."

I suggest, however, that if we define the overall conception of the poem in Joyce's terms as a collection of epiphanies several perplexing problems may be resolved. To begin with we can recognize that it contains a number of epiphanic moments but is not pure epiphany, which is another way of saying that Whitman's theory of poetry is very much like Eliot's in its insistence on preserving those "impurities" which prevent the movement to a symbolism so extreme that content disappears. The dynamic of Whitman's poem may be described as an alternation of discursive sections with those in which the epiphany is exposed. These discursive sections may be likened to the natural facts, which frame, introduce, or sometimes through sheer accumulation bring the epiphanic moment into being. Whitman uses the discursive passages in a variety of ways, but two are of special interest here. They provide the basis for the central narrative framework of the poem which derives from a rather conventional personal autobiography, though of course the persona in the poem is a representative man in purely Emersonian terms. But the point is that there is a precise narrative outline, a first person point of view which announces at the outset: "I celebrate myself,/ And what I assume you shall assume,/ For every atom belonging to me as good belongs to you." Whitman fills us in with other relevant information and occasionally gives exposition of antecedent action: "Born here of parents born here from parents the same, and their parents the same,/ I, now thirty-seven years old in perfect health begin,/ hoping to cease not till death"; and later, he gives us the first mention of his name, which did not appear on the title page of the first edition, "Walt Whitman, an American, one of the roughs."

A second use of the discursive sections is to present major statements of Whitman's ideology. The political ideology has been well noted, but Whitman uses this device as a means of explaining his esthetic as well. Thus in one of the Inscriptions he gives us a nice statement of his poetic approach:

Poets to come! orators, singers, musicians to come!
Not to-day is to justify me and answer what I am for,
But you, a new brood, native, athletic, continental greater than
before known,
Arouse! for you must justify me.

I myself but write one or two indicative words for the future,
I but advance a moment only to wheel and hurry back in the
darkness.
I am a man who, sauntering along without fully stopping, turns a
casual look upon you and then averts his face,
Leaving it to you to prove and define it,
Expecting the main things from you.

If we put this in the framework of Emerson's theory we can recognize several familiar ideas. The indicative words remind us of the theory of symbols and the limits of language, which can show us the path to truth, but only indirectly (through metaphor) and with centuple meanings which ultimately merge into the darkness. The poet gives a hint but without fully stopping, for he knows the limits of full explication of language, and hence averts his face leaving the rest to the reader. As in Joyce (who resembles Whitman very closely in this respect) we need to look carefully to discover that the passage works in more than one direction. But there can be no doubt that Whitman was anxious for the reader to learn the method whereby poems are made, and he tells us in "Song of Myself":

Stop this day and night with me and you shall possess the origin
of all poems,
You shall possess the good of the earth and sun, (there are
millions of suns left),
You shall no longer take things at second or third hand, nor look
through the eyes of the dead, nor feed on spectres in books,
You shall not look through my eyes either, nor take things from
me,
You shall listen to all sides and filter them from yourself.

Similarly we find his statement of the relationship between the body and the soul (a major motif to which I shall return) as an analogue to the symbolic process: "Clear and sweet is my soul, and clear and sweet is all that is not my soul./ Lack one lacks both, and the unseen is proved by the seen,/ Till that becomes unseen and receives proof in its turn." To prove the unseen from the seen is in effect to move from natural facts to spiritual truths, and it is notable that Whitman, like Emerson, recognizes that the symbol is vehicular rather than static, resulting in a sense of process rather than ultimate truth. It is for this reason that Whitman is often related to the symbolist tradition, but, as I have pointed out, he is not capable of moving toward the final stage of art for art's sake or pure poetry. Hence while Charles Feidelson, Jr., is surely right in relating Whitman's approach to symbolish techniques, he is misleading when he suggests that Whitman was a Valéry *manqué*: "Since Whitman regards meaning as an activity of words rather than an external significance attached to them, language, together with the self and the material world, turns out to be a process, the pouring of the flood." On the one hand, Whitman could not go all the way in his symbolist approach; on the other hand, he has neither the architectural stability of a writer like Hawthorne nor the curbing skepticism of Melville: "Whatever the nominal subject, it is soon lost in sheer 'process'; all roads lead into the 'Song of Myself,' in which the bare ego interacts with a miscellaneous world. The result is Whitman's characteristic disorder and turgidity. When the subject is endless, any form becomes arbitrary."[12]

But Whitman does not use language as an end in itself or as an antagonist to content. Language, as we have already seen, is one part of the system whereby the epiphany may be produced, but it cannot function without the mediating element of natural facts. Thus, unlike Joyce, and in the tradition which I have identified with Emerson's esthetic, Whitman provides both the sense of process and a clear commitment to content for its own sake. Before we can make value judgments about this approach, we need to be sure that it is not confused with something that Whitman did not intend it to be. We seem to be in a Joycean world because Whitman moves into the epiphanic sections without providing clear narrative transitions, just as Eliot does in *The Waste Land*. (Ezra Pound, as we know, was Eliot's editor; Whitman, however, was his own editor and achieved a similar effect.) But the overall effect is clearly an alternation of narrative with epiphanic passages. In the latter, we do seem to be involved in something like a stream of consciousness (or subconsciousness) that reminds us of Joyce in sections of *Ulysses* or *Finnegans Wake,* and aside from noting the similarities, this comparison is worth making because we can then see that Whitman is as highly organized and controlled in "Song of Myself" as Joyce was in his work. (It is tantalizing to recall Buck Mulligan's response to Stephen Dedalus's chiding in *Ulysses*:

"Contradiction. Do I contradict myself? Very well then, I contradict myself.") How many epiphanic passages there are is a question that ought to be left open. Whitman can sometimes achieve the effect in a small compass; but there are several major sections which I think can best be explained in the way I have suggested. The first is the best known; it picks up the motif I noted earlier in connection with the relationship between the body and the soul:

> I believe in you my soul, the other I am must not abase itself to
>   you,
> And you must not be abased to the other.
>
> Loafe with me on the grass, loose the stop from your throat,
> Not words, not music or rhyme I want, not custom or lecture, not
>   even the best,
> Only the lull I like, the hum of your valvèd voice.
>
> I mind how once we lay such a transparent summer morning,
> How you settled your head athwart my hips and gently turn'd
>   over upon me,
> And parted the shirt from my bosom-bone, and plunged your
>   tongue to my bare-strip heart,
> And reached till you felt my beard, and reached till you held my
>   feet.
>
> Swiftly arose and spread around me the peace and knowledge
>   that pass all the argument of the earth,
> And I know that the hand of God is the promise of my own,
> And I know that the spirit of God is the brother of my own,
> And that all the men ever born are also my brothers, and the
>   women my sisters and lovers,
> And that a kelson of the creation is love,
> And limitless are leaves stiff or drooping in the fields,
> And brown ants in the little wells beneath them,
> And mossy scabs of the worm fence, heap'd stones, elder, mullein
>   and poke weed.

I suggest that there is little virtue in searching for the real experience upon which this passage may be based, if by that we mean the actual occasion on which Whitman engaged in sexual activity with his girl-friend, boyfriend, or himself. No such momentous occasion has been identified—and indeed there may in fact have been none, or a dozen. But I think we are on safer ground if we stay closer to the text and note that Whitman gives us a dialogue between the body and the soul in an attempt to formulate in a basically Emersonian manner the relationship between matter and spirit. Such dialogues are actually rather conventional in English literature and often use a similar sexual metaphor to dramatize the interaction. It is clearly the soul which is being addressed and invited to loaf on the grass and what Whitman wants from it is the power of expression, a level of speech far above mere music, rhyme, custom or lecture (all of these are close descriptions of the conventional literature which both Emerson and Whitman attacked). If we keep this in conventional terms, it is inspiration Whitman desires, that underlying source of poetic power which even words cannot contain but which he describes as the lull, the hum of the soul's valvèd voice. The term valvèd may refer to the loosing of the stop, transforming its expression into something smoother and freer, though at the same time it suggests something of a valved instrument like a trumpet or perhaps even better a trombone with its swooping and absolutely chromatic possibilities.

The next segment is still a description of the intercourse between body and soul and aside from the unabashedly sexual imagery it may be taken as precisely like Emerson's experience on the common in twilight. It is the soul who lies with the poet that summer morning, its head on his lap, then turns to part the shirt and plunge its tongue to his heart. The relationship of tongue to heart continues the idea that the soul will provide expression for the body, giving voice to its material existence. But while this is similar to Emerson's experience the difference is that Whitman places the experience in the context of language and the symbolic power that it gives the poet, while Emerson characteristically makes a general, discursive statement. Emerson is essentially the essayist while Whitman gives us a poetic statement and we become aware not only of the content but the form as well, most notably in the superb sound of "Only the lull I like, the hum of your valvèd voice," which as numerous critics have acknowledged is as good a line as can be found in any poet. But the implications of the passage are Emersonian as Whitman makes clear the essential role of the physical in relation to the spiritual. The union of the body and the soul are equivalent to the necessity for the poet to work with both the understanding and the reason. Spiritual truth cannot be achieved by eliminating the material but only by going through it. Hence the appropriateness of the sexual imagery comes into focus. Whitman's theme is the creative power of the poet and the sexual act is not only the traditional but also the logical means by which it may be expressed. Indeed the act of coitus, which begins with physical stimulation, may literally bring the participants to a state of spiritual ecstasy. We can recall Whitman's habitual reference to his poems as seminal excrescenses; "Cushion me soft," he says to the sea, "rock me in billowy drowse,/ Dash me with amorous wet, I can repay you." And in "Children of Adam" he uses the same image:

I, chanter of Adamic songs,
Through the new garden the West, the great cities calling,
Deliriate, thus prelude what is generated, offering these, offering
    myself,
Bathing myself, bathing my songs in Sex,
Offspring of my loins.

These last lines are in the narrative mode, but the section under discussion renders the scene dramatically and forces the reader to catch the connotations and the nuances of the symbolism. We can see then that there is no confusion about Whitman's position: he is an idealist but like Emerson he recognizes that spiritual truth may be achieved only through the physical and through the agency of symbolic language. (As to *sexual position* in the passage, it is the soul's tongue to the body's heart—and nothing more.)

If we look closely we discover that even the most shockingly materialistic acclamations are only repetitions of this view. The most outrageous expression for Whitman's early readers still troubles many of his contemporary critics:

I accept Reality and dare not question it,
Materialism first and last imbuing.

Hurrah for positive science! long live exact demonstration!
Fetch stonecrop mixt with cedar and branches of lilac,
This is the lexicographer, this the chemist, this made a grammar
    of the old cartouches,
These mariners put the ship through dangerous unknown seas,
This is the geologist, this works with the scalpel, and this is a
    mathematician.

I find it hard to understand how any reader can miss the obvious humor of these lines which exemplify the truth of Richard Chase's assertion that the essential mode of "Song of Myself" is comedy. The tone is one that we often hear in Whitman and it must have been passages like this that Henry James delighted in declaiming at the top of his voice. (There are many others equally funny in which Whitman combines levels of diction to undercut conventional morality and the sense of genteel behavior—like suddenly shrieking in the midst of afternoon tea: "Undrape! you are not guilty to me, nor stale nor discarded"; "Unscrew the locks from the doors!/ Unscrew the doors themselves from their jambs"; "I speak the pass-word primeval, I give the sign of democracy,/By God! I will accept nothing which all cannot have their counterpart of on the same terms"; "You there, impotent, loose in the knees,/ Open your scarf'd chops till I blow grit within you.") But we cannot miss the implications of what immediately follows this cheer for the exact sciences: "Gentlemen, to you the first honors always!/ Your facts are useful, and yet they are not my dwelling,/ I but enter by them to an area of my dwelling."

The physical union of the body and the soul leads to the final statement of the epiphany, a vision of brotherhood and peace couched in terms that suggest Old Testament promises. The highest level of sexuality is spiritual love, or to put it in Emersonian terms, sex is the natural fact which, through the use of symbolism, will reveal the spiritual truth—love of mankind. The overall form of the passage may be sketched thus: a statement of the theme (the relationship of body to soul); dramatization of the union in sexual terms; evocation of the spiritual truth; and a final catalogue of natural facts which brings us back to the level of the understanding. It is at the same time an example of what Whitman means by indirection. The meaning of the passage becomes clear only through close analysis, revealing its import through the images that define the epiphanic experience. There is no preaching, no shrieking, and, after the thematic statement, the mode is not discursive but symbolist in its communication. Only gradually does it reveal itself to us and when Whitman is done he passes on to the next section with no transition.

One of Whitman's great accomplishments is his ability to use sex thematically in his poetry. It got him into trouble and still creates difficulties for his readers, for often Whitman uses sex purely for its shock value as when he constantly threatens to remove his clothes or insists: "The scent of these arm-pits aroma finer than prayer." But beyond this, sex is almost always the natural fact which symbolizes the spiritual truth, defined as love or the creative power of the poet, and Whitman was quite conscious of its thematic implications, as a passage in *A Backward Glance* reveals: "From another point of view 'Leaves of Grass' is avowedly the song of Sex and Amativeness, and even Animality—though meanings that do not usually go along with those words are behind all, and will duly emerge; and all are sought to be lifted into a different light and atmosphere. . . . Difficult as it will be, it has become, in my opinion, imperative to achieve a shifted attitude from superior men and women towards the thought and fact of sexuality, as an element in character, personality, the emotions, and a theme in literature." D. H. Lawrence, in his celebrated essay, caught just this strategy noting: "The essential function of art is moral. Not aesthetic, not decorative, not pastime and recreation . . . but a passionate, implicit morality, not didactic. . . . Now Whitman was a great moralist. He was a great leader. He was a great changer of the blood in the veins of men. Surely it is especially true of American art, that it is all essentially moral. Hawthorne, Poe, Longfellow, Emerson, Melville: it is the moral issue which engages them. They all feel uneasy about the old morality. Sensuously, passionally, they all attack the old morality. But they know nothing better, mentally. Therefore they give tight mental allegiance to a morality which all their passion goes to destroy. Hence the duplicity which is the fatal flaw in them . . . tight mental allegiance given to a morality which the passional self repudiates. Whitman was the first to break the mental allegiance. He was the first to smash the old moral conception, that the soul of man is something 'superior' and 'above' the flesh. Even Emerson still maintained this tiresome 'superiority' of the soul. Even Melville could not get over it. Whitman was the first heroic seer to seize the soul by the scruff of her neck and plant her down among the potsherds."[13] Whitman's approach to the body and the soul is essentially Emersonian, though Lawrence is correct in noting that Whitman broke ground in this respect, ridding himself of the paralyzing dichotomy between matter and spirit. And yet we need to emphasize Lawrence's awareness that Whitman is a moralist though not didactic. I think that Lawrence means by passionate, implicit morality the ability to give us the concrete image from which the moral truth flows—which is precisely the mark of Emerson's esthetic and to a large extent that of American poetry in general.

Though it is not possible to map all the epiphanies in the poem (or even desirable to push the thesis I have proposed to mechanical applications) it will be worthwhile to look at another one which is similar to the epiphany in section five:

To behold the day-break!
The little light fades the immense and diaphanous shadows,
The air tastes good to my palate.

Hefts of the moving world at innocent gambols silently rising,
    freshly exuding,
Scooting, obliquely high and low.

Something I cannot see puts upward libidinous prongs,
Seas of bright juice suffuse heaven.

The earth by the sky staid with, the daily close of their junction,
The heav'd challenge from the east that moment over my head,
The mocking taunt. See then whether you shall be master.

Here the moment is sunrise and we can recognize a conventional
topic of poetry as well as the visual arts. The natural fact is daybreak
and as often is the case with Whitman we can find ourselves in the
position of trying to guess what spiritual truth it will lead us to. (That
is, I am referring back to the passage I quoted earlier in which Whitman writes a few indicative words, leaving the rest to us.) He performs
what we have come to recognize as an essential task of the poet by
making new what can easily become a trite though universal occurrence. To do so means breaking away from stereotyped attitudes
toward nature and language, especially the sense of awe and respect
which one comes to expect in this genre. It is a new vision of something which is commonplace as well as archetypal, and it necessitates
looking at the phenomenon with eyes unclouded either by literary
tradition or artificial models. We might say again, to see the miraculous
in the commonplace but an example of a different approach to a
natural scene may make the point better: "We were overshadowed
by lofty trees, with straight, smooth trunks, like stately columns; and
as the glancing rays of the sun shone through the transparent leaves,
tinted with the many-colored hues of autumn, I was reminded of the
effect of sunshine among the stained windows and clustering columns
of a Gothic cathedral. Indeed there is a grandeur and solemnity in
our spacious forests of the West, that awakens in me the same feeling
I have experienced in those vast and venerable piles, and the sound
of the wind sweeping through them supplies occasionally the deep
breathings of the organ." This passage is from Washington Irving's
A Tour on the Prairies (1835) and it is the more significant because
it is based on actual observations that Irving made on his trip. But it
is interesting to note that Irving saw this Western scene through the
filters of literary convention, and we may doubt whether he was
capable of seeing it at all. The frame of reference and the language it
evokes remove us from the forest itself in an attempt to raise the
scene to a level of high culture. The allusions are significantly to
European artifacts, hence the trunks become "stately columns" as in
classical architecture; the forest itself is a Gothic cathedral—the architectural combination is difficult to visualize except as it might appear in Dali's surrealistic mélanges, an effect that Irving would not

have relished. The effect he was after, however, is clearly stated. It awakened the sense of "grandeur and solemnity" in the face of nature which one experiences in the presence of a church, and thus Irving confesses to an essentially religious feeling which quite effectively frames the world of nature in a category that will contain its identity in more controllable terms. That is, man is reminded of his smallness and humility in the presence of God, the Great Organist. The language operates on a similar level of abstraction: lofty trees, smooth trunks, many-colored hues, vast and venerable piles. Irving's critics have noted that he was less condescending than most of his contemporaries who visited the West, and we must admit that his artistry and ideology are in excellent accord.

But if we return to Whitman's passage the extent of his accomplishment is apparent. It depends on several techniques that show how careful Whitman could be in his use of language, which is not at all "folksy" or consciously low diction. (Only "scooting" and "juice" might strike us as notable.) The major effect comes from the submerged sexual metaphor in which the dawn is made analogous to an orgasm: "Something I cannot see puts upward libidinous prongs,/ Seas of bright juice suffuse heaven." The junction of earth and sky is a cosmic intercourse very like those which appear in Middle Eastern myth. (Something which Whitman might easily have known.) But his interest is not in allusions to Egyptology. Each sunrise is a fresh act of creation, each day is like the first day, and the motif reminds us of Emerson's comment in *Nature* that "To speak truly, few adult persons can see nature. Most persons do not see the sun. At least they have a very superficial seeing." Only those whose "inward and outward senses are still truly adjusted to each other" can be understood to have real perception. To see nature fully is to recognize that the natural fact is a symbol of the spiritual truth.

And in the lines immediately following, Whitman draws the inference, which by this time we can ourselves predict: "Dazzling and tremendous how quick the sun-rise would kill me, If I could not now and always send sun-rise out of me." As in the earlier section, the sexual imagery is the symbol of the poet's creative power and it is again seen in the context of language: "My voice goes after what my eyes cannot reach,/ With the twirl of my tongue I encompass worlds and volumes of worlds." But we should not be misled by the connotations of Whitman's images into thinking that the creative process is simply a jetting forth of language indiscriminately. Whitman often liked to give this impression and we can understand the strategy as part of the role he assumed in order to shock genteel sensibilities. It is what I shall define later as an essential approach in American humor, closely related to the Arkansas Traveler motif, in which the American consciously assumes the character of a barbarian in order to undercut European stereotypes. But it is only partly a role; in another sense Whitman brings us to an awareness of the aboriginal experience still available to men even within the framework of civilization. His approach to nature is thus neither "romantic" nor simply allusive. Rather it shows the validity of Emerson's theory that concrete observation of natural facts is the channel which leads to universal, spiritual truths. Whitman is at his best when he implements this technique, but there are moments when the balance between natural facts and spiritual truths is lost and then his poems become too concrete or disturbingly abstract. "Song of Myself," however, represents Whitman's highest accomplishment ideologically as well as artistically. With the aid of Emerson's theory of language and in the context of a folk ideology whose lineage goes back to Herder he became truly the father of his nation's poetic tradition and with a subtlety that raised the entire meaning of folk literature to a level higher than anyone could have suspected. Whitman's ability to use sex thematically follows closely Emerson's prediction that the symbol will be more pungent if it relies on archetypal sources, and it foreshadows a similar consequence in the use of the blues as a literary theme.

The extent of Whitman's subtlety has become increasingly acknowledged by recent critics.[14] Asselineau notes that, "The impression of ease or 'abandon,' as he said, which Whitman's work gives, was, in fact, the result of careful planning. His simplicity is laboured, and that is why he approved the famous line of Ben Jonson: 'good poet's made as well as born.' The first version of Leaves of Grass, far from having been written at one sitting, evolved slowly from a considerable number of drafts of the kind which Emory Holloway has published and which represent the work of several years. The short poems of his old age required as much trouble. There exist at the Library of Congress ten different drafts of 'Supplement Hours.' "[15] Asselineau concludes that Whitman's characteristic mode of composition was "agglutinative." That is to say, the poems "were composed like mosaics and, as in mosaics, a number of lines or passages are interchangeable. Whitman himself, in the course of the successive editions, did not hesitate to change the order of certain paragraphs." It makes it possible for Asselineau to explain effectively the overall looseness of Leaves of Grass. In "Song of Myself," however, this quality of mosaic brings to mind the formulaic technique of folk tradition which employs precisely the same approach in standardized epithets and situations. Whitman's principled rejection of traditional epic forms prevented him from following such stock techniques. Moreover, as most of his critics are forced to admit sooner or later, the standard conceptions of architectural structure will not encompass Whitman's accomplishments. The main explanations for Whitman's form (that it was mystically given to him in its entirety, or that there simply is not any) have been fairly well discounted. But the question still remains vexed because of an assumption that is still widely held and applied to all the main figures of nineteenth-century American literature, as well as some who appear later. It is that Americans, having lost the sense of connection with Old World traditions will inevitably face a crisis in the formal development of their art. Certainly such writers as Hawthorne and James have openly admitted that they found themselves in such circumstances. But I think Whitman's achievement shows that a rejection of some formal approaches of earlier tradition did not mean he was left with no resources. It is true, however, that the isolation of many American writers (including Whitman) from the mainstream of English and European tradition must be seen as a special pressure that led toward the inventing of new forms, some of which, as I have already suggested, anticipated contemporary literary approaches. I have defined his main technique as an alternation of narrative and epiphanic sections, which enabled Whitman to exploit the fullest range of his ideological and esthetic resources. Taken in the context of his sensitivity to the possibilities of language, his awareness of the national and international implications of literature, his absolute conviction that creative power was innate in mankind and not the result of genteel conventions—taking all this into account, it does not seem necessary to impose any more rigorous standards upon Whitman's work. The test of a style is that it can express itself easily and effectively in its own terms. As Meyer Schapiro has defined the term, style refers "to the constant form—and sometimes the constant elements, qualities and expression—in the art of an individual or a group. . . . But the style is, above all, a system of forms with a quality and a meaningful expression through which the personality of the artist and the broad outlook of a group are visible. It is also a vehicle of expression within the group, communicating and fixing certain values of religious, social, and moral life through the emotional suggestiveness of forms. It is, besides, a common ground against which innovation and the individuality of particular works may be measured."[16] If Whitman's critics have missed these qualities in his work, it is because they fail to take into account another dictum which Schapiro emphasizes in his formulation: "There is no privileged content or mode of representation (although the greatest works may, for reasons obscure to us, occur only in certain styles). Perfect art is possible in any subject matter or style. A style is like a language, with an internal order and expressiveness, admitting a varied intensity or delicacy of statement. This approach is a relativism that does not exclude absolute judgments of value; it makes these judgments possible within every framework by abandoning a fixed norm of style. Such ideas are accepted by most students of art today, although not applied with uniform conviction." And it seems to me that in this respect Whitman was more sophisticated in his insights than most of his critics. He understood very well the limits of language for complete or absolute expression, recalling perhaps as Emerson did that the recourse to figurative language was itself a definition of the human condition. He was in full accord with Emerson's dictum that the symbol was "vehicular" and good for conveyance rather than homestead. That is what he meant by the expression, "easily written loose finger'd chords," and we shall see how close that brings us to similar approaches which find a major source of literary form in folksong, blues, and jazz. At the same time, Whitman constantly reminds us in his text that his approach will be radical. "Not words of outline this song of mine," he says, "But abruptly to question, to leap beyond yet nearer bring." What is annoying and sometimes infuriating to many of Whitman's readers and critics is the audacity and lack of decorum that often informs his tone; but that is only so if we forget the folk ideology underlying Whitman's remarks. Randall Jarrell has hit the mark in proposing for the poet's tombstone: "WALT WHITMAN: HE HAD HIS NERVE." But it was the same Whitman who insisted, in words reminiscent of the folk hymn, "Lonesome Valley": "Not I, not anyone else can travel that road for you,/ You must travel it for yourself." It is an egotism for the world that Whitman proposes, maintaining, "(It is you talking just as much as myself, I act as the tongue of you,/ Tied in your mouth, in mine it begins to be loosen'd.)." For the ultimate source of his strategy we need to turn to American folk tradition.

Chapter Four
Folklore and
the American Character

THE QUESTION of form in relation to American literature has almost always been framed in ideological terms. That is, the critics who find American writers deficient in matters of formal analysis have identified this failure as the result of America's isolation from the historic developments of European literature. Underlying what appears to be an essentially esthetic evaluation is the central conception that America is simply too young and too vulgar to have developed a meaningful and effective esthetic. This is the substance of Santayana's critique of Whitman, who is associated with what Santayana calls "the poetry of barbarism." Although Whitman is granted a certain vitality, "It is in the rebellion against discipline, in the abandonment of the ideals of classic and Christian tradition, that this rejuvenation is found. . . . For the barbarian is the man who regards his passions as their own excuse for being; who does not domesticate them either by understanding their cause or by conceiving their ideal goal. He is the man who does not know his derivations nor perceive his tendencies, but who merely feels and acts, valuing in his life its force and its filling, but being careless of its purpose and form."[1] The elements of this critique are familiar and appear in a variety of contexts. Philip Rahv's widely quoted characterization moves along the same lines: "Viewed historically, American writers appear to group themselves around two popular types. Paleface and redskin I should like to call the two, and despite occasional efforts at reconciliation no love is lost between them." According to Rahv, "the creative mind in America is fragmented and one-sided. For the process of polarization has produced a dichotomy between experience and consciousness—a dissociation between energy and sensibility, between life conceived as an opportunity and life conceived as a discipline."[2] Whitman is the classic instance of the redskin as James is the exemplar of the paleface, and indeed almost anyone can then fill in his own illustration of the two sides which define American literature. There are in this formulation several unexpressed assumptions which are germane to the issues I have been discussing and I think that approaching them within the framework of my analysis may provide some fresh insights, though hardly any final solutions.

Two of these issues are clearly folkloristic and I propose to look at them in the context of Constance Rourke's approach to the folk sources of American literature. With one exception, very little analysis of her method and approach has appeared since her death in 1941.[3] In an otherwise sympathetic essay, Stanley Edgar Hyman found her work flawed because, unlike Jane Harrison, Miss Rourke did not follow the clues in her materials to their ultimate source in myth and ritual. It is a little like criticizing Mark Twain because he was not William Shakespeare. Her interests, that is, lay in other directions, and with the publication of *American Humor, A Study of the National Character* (1931) Miss Rourke focused her attention on two major issues: the folk sources of an American literary tradition, and the function of humor in its development. In her reliance on Herderian ideology and her major concern with the American writer's response to traditional notions of genres, Miss Rourke has made a major contribution to our understanding of the American identity and its reflection in our literature.

Constance Rourke's first preoccupation in *American Humor* was to offset the assertion by many of her contemporaries that American civilization had little to offer in the fine arts. The history of this assumption is long and complicated, but as we have seen, one of its major formulations (reinforced from time to time by native as well as foreign critics) is based on the notion that the United States was brought into existence under circumstances that denied it the period of gestation necessary for the creation of a mature and richly textured culture. The unexpressed assumption in this argument she understood as essentially Herderian. What it really meant to say was that no nation can create a formal, fine art tradition unless it has a folk culture to build it upon. If there is a distinctive literary tradition in this country, she argued, there must have been a matrix of folk and popular materials behind it. Later, in *The Roots of American Culture* (1942) she specifically identified this view with the philosophy of Herder, especially his view that a nation's literature is truly national and legitimately its own when it arises from the folklore of its people. Denied a feudal era, America apparently lacked just such a crucial period of folk accumulation which, in Herder's conception, was necessary to the building of an indigenous literature. As a result, Miss Rourke pointed out, the idea that America was a derivative (and therefore inferior) culture "was inevitably accepted in the colonial era and has been further defined, elaborated and added to explicitly or otherwise until it stands as a main approach to the study of our culture and even our political, social and economic history."[4] What small reservoir of folklore might be found here was the result of emigration from the Old World, the colonists naturally bringing with them the forms of their native folk traditions. But this would provide little in the way of nourishment for an American folklore. "The arts would spread much as water is passed in buckets at a country fire," she explained, "—spilled along the way no doubt, with much of it lost and perhaps acquiring a peculiar tang of flavor, if one should taste it. What we might hope eventually to possess was an extension of European culture, that is, if the process of diffusion was not too greatly impaired by forces peculiar to American life."[5] Here was the rub, for not only was it asserted that America had not created its own folk tradition, it was also argued that any meaningful importations would be vitiated by the American experience.

The first task in any correction of this view was to establish the nature and significance of those conditions and materials in America which could provide the basis of a national literature. In an earlier work, Miss Rourke had employed folklore decoratively to enliven the basic outlines of her story.[6] But in *American Humor* she developed a method of literary and cultural analysis which was, in the strictest sense, neither folkloristic nor historical, but a unique combination of disciplines. "This book," she wrote in the foreword, "has no quarrel with the American character; one might as well dispute with some established feature in the natural landscape. Nor can it be called a defense. . . . This study has grown from an enjoyment of American vagaries, and from the belief that these have woven together a tradition which is various, subtle, sinewy, scant at times but not poor."[7] Despite its relatively short existence, Miss Rourke insisted, America had its own tradition, unique in its development and rich enough to control and color the flow of formal art which issued from it.

In the first of what was to be a trio of characterological studies, Miss Rourke discerned the lineaments of the American as they emerged in the figure of the Yankee. By the end of the eighteenth century, she noted, he was easily identified as the peddler, a lone, shrewd figure who had already become more than regional, taking on aspects of myth and fantasy. It was an image fashioned, as it is to this day, by New England, the West, and even the South. The emphasis on the finagling, calculating merchant (strangely analogous to the stereotype of the Jew) obscured origins that were complex and variegated. Puritanism may have provided body to the Yankee myth, but to Miss Rourke's eye it contained too dark a view to be responsible for his fanciful humor and irreverence. There was folklore indeed in seventeenth-century New England, but it ran to witchery and the grotesque, which led Miss Rourke to suggest that "humor bears the closest relation to emotion, either bubbling up as from a deep and happy wellspring, or in the opposite fashion rising like a re-birth of feeling from dead levels of turmoil" (*American Humor,* p. 20). The Yankee rebounded from the deep but compressed emotion of Puritanism, retaining from those early experiences mainly the use of the mask, what she referred to as a "portable heirloom." In response to the restrictions of Puritan rule and as a means of blunting the starkness of pioneer existence, the persona became a permanent part of the Yankee's make-up. Similar traits of swapping and dissembling might be traced to the Yorkshireman, but Miss Rourke emphasized the mixing of strains from other sections of the British Isles and even France. The background was complex and she was neither simplistic nor provincial in her evaluation of its sources.

Her discussion of the seventeenth century was sparse, for although there were distinct outlines of permanent influence in the life and thought of the period, it was the Revolutionary War era which, "with its cutting of ties, its movement, its impulses toward freedom, seemed to set one portion of the scant population free from its narrow matrix" (*American Humor,* p. 21). Just at this point, when the Yankee began to emerge as a national symbol, Miss Rourke noted also the emergence of a major theme in American cultural history and a characteristic literary strategy. The tension between Europe and America, which later critics have identified as the "international theme," is apparent from the very beginning of our national history. Miss Rourke was rarely a polemicist, but in a bibliographical note at the end of *American Humor* she criticized Van Wyck Brooks for not recognizing that "the international scene is a natural and even traditional subject." The insight was a crucial one for it illuminated a problem that many critics had either overlooked or misinterpreted. The contrast between Europe and America (especially between England and the United States) in politics, manners, and literary theory led some scholars to place the conflict outside the configurations of American experience. The nature as well as the significance of the antagonism were thus easily misread as manifestations of American chauvinism or British pomposity. By placing the opposition of Old World and New squarely in the mainstream of American thought, Miss Rourke skirted the pitfalls of either extreme position, at the same time affirming its significance as an American rather than a strictly regional antagonism. Much of the criticism leveled by both sides was accurate. But the important point, she insisted, was that the American character was formed under the pressure of criticism from abroad, a circumstance which helped to explain some of its special qualities and the literary strategies in which it was represented. (In a later section of *American Humor* she identified the international theme as a major one in the work of both Mark Twain and Henry James.)

Throughout the early decades of the nineteenth century the Yankee proved a fertile source for journalistic, theatrical, and literary productions. Even in the West, frontier folk found it possible to identify with the Easterner in the face of persistent attacks by the British. The Yankee's major virtue was adaptability, his main accomplishment the creation of a subtle humor, couched not so much in a new dialect as in a new "lingo." (The distinction is James Russell Lowell's and Miss Rourke interpreted it to mean that "its oddities of language were consciously assumed.") Yet the Yankee remained a highly complex character who operated most effectively on the level of fantasy, a stratagem which managed to keep secretive the innermost qualities of his mind and personality: "The Yankee was never passive, not the crackerbox philosopher seated in some dim interior, uttering wisdom before a ring of quiet figures; he was noticeably out in the world; it was a prime part of his character to be 'a-doin'.' . . . Though he talked increasingly his monologues still never brimmed over into personal revelation. He was drawn with ample color and circumstance, yet he was not wholly a person. His mask, so simply and blankly worn, had closed down without a crack or a seam to show a glimpse of the human creature underneath" (*American Humor*, p. 34). The failure to develop the Yankee into a minutely observed personality Miss Rourke saw as a triumph rather than a shortcoming, for it signified a "concerted interest in another direction." The character's appearance in tales, fables, and plays suggested the creation of a mythical figure, and even at this early period, a movement away from the realistic portraiture associated with the English novel. Myth here means "an ideal image, a self-image, one of those symbols which peoples spontaneously adopt and by which in some measure they live." There were, in fact, elements of the demigod in this creation, but Miss Rourke identified as a controlling gesture the tendency "toward the upset of old and rigid balances"; his comic sense attacked the old values, as indeed the conflict with the British had already suggested. It is another intimation of the curious fact that in American tradition folklore seems to co-exist with radical ideologies rather than to affirm the old conservative values, as antiquarian folklorists have emphasized. In the process, however, the figure of the Yankee foreshadowed the American. His basic qualities of adaptability, self-confidence, and vitality were the result of a hybridization of diverse forms. The Yankee presented an outline which was filled in during the course of American development.

The second major phase of this steady accretion of national characteristics bore the clear imprint of the backwoodsman. Miss Rourke noted the interesting fact that as the Yankee had emerged from the embroilments of the Revolutionary War, so the frontiersman made his appearance during the War of 1812. In both cases the pressure of a military and political conflict demanded a forceful image capable of fusing diverse aspects of the national imagination. But a more significant insight is her insistence that the backwoodsman's ancestry was similar to the Yankee's, rooted in Calvinism and drawing upon the same ethnic stocks. His response to the wilderness was more extreme than the Yankee's reaction to the New England frontier: "Strength was his obsession—size, scale, power: he seemed obliged to shout their symbols as if after all he were not wholly secure in their possession. . . . He shouted in ritual, as though the emotions by which he was moved were bending him to some primitive celebration. . . . They even appeared, in the fertile new country, like those primitive ceremonies to produce growth by which the sower leaps high to make the hemp grow high" (*American Humor*, p. 40). The movement was toward the same goal marked out by the Yankee, the process consisting mainly of filling in the earlier outline. Miss Rourke's emphasis here is upon the influence of the new land upon an already identifiable new man. He created a new bestiary, including mythical animals, drawing freely upon the lore and legend of Indians and Negro slaves. Indeed a new folk music arose through his "mixing Negro breakdowns with Irish reels and jigs," and in his singing "his rough improvisations mingled with the older songs." But the crowning accomplishment was the backwoodsman himself, "a new beast" spawned by the rivers and forests of the West. Miss Rourke was fully aware of the implications held by her descriptions of this new stage in the synthesis of old and new elements. There was a dark stain at the heart of this development. Horror, terror, and death were ever present in the frontier experience; the tales and legends of the frontiersman repeated an earlier motif which mingled magical outcroppings of birth with clear intimations of terror and death, resulting often in a middle ground that Miss Rourke identified as the grotesque. In all this, however, the comic sense functioned as before, providing a resilience which "swept through them in waves, transcending the past, transcending terror, with the sense of comedy itself a wild emotion."

The actors in this part of the unfolding drama of creation were diverse and flamboyant, uniting in their own persons the elements of reality and the fantastic. They include Davy Crockett, Mike Fink, Ben Hardin and a host of literary creations who heralded the conscious evocation of a native American humor. Crockett became a demigod, his birth attributed to supernatural agencies, his real death incapable of stemming the continuing profusion of stories recounting his incredible and heroic exploits. In one famous tale, which Miss Rourke recounts, Crockett rescues the earth from oblivion through a Promethean effort that frees the sun from its frozen axes. The manipulation of his popularity by the political enemies of Andrew Jackson only temporarily diverted attention from the mythical implications of his life and adventures. Mike Fink was "a Mississippi river-god, one of those minor deities whom men create in their own image and magnify to magnify themselves" (*American Humor,* p. 53). The exploits of the flatboatmen never attained the widespread circulation of the Crockett tales, but Mike Fink passed into oral tradition, "achieving the final glory of heroes, a death wrapped in mystery, indeed many deaths, for the true story was lost, and others sprang up" (*American Humor,* p. 53). This was important documentation for Miss Rourke's argument that a usable folk tradition did indeed exist in this country.

One of her major methodological accomplishments is exemplified in her ability to identify the juxtaposition of folk and popular traditions within which the American character developed. Folklore exposes the deepest level of national traits and values; it is an anonymous tradition rooted in oral story telling and is passed down from person to person until the layers of truth and fiction become one, indistinguishable from each other. Popular art exists on a more conscious level, often utilizing folk themes but easily recognizable as the work of a particular individual. She saw more clearly than any other critic the peculiar tendency in America for folk and popular traditions to merge rather than to exist separately in isolated areas, as is often the case in Europe. We discover often a figure so close to folk tradition that he can recreate on a popular level what seems essentially folk in its style. Mark Twain and Woody Guthrie are of this sort, and so was James Audubon, whose ornithology Miss Rourke related to the huntsman's close knowledge of nature. Audubon not only adopted the backwoodsman's flair for costume and disguise; he also invented mythical species of birds and fish, including the "Devil-Jack-Diamond-Fish that grew to be ten feet in length and was armored with large stone scales of diamond shape set in oblique rows, which were bullet-proof, and which when dried would strike fire with steel" (*American Humor,* p. 50). On a similar level, the work of Southwestern humorists brought into existence a group of characters— Simon Suggs, Sut Lovingood, Major Jones and others most fully exemplified in Longstreet's *Georgia Scenes*—whose irreverence and grotesqueries provided a "portraiture of new types in the new country." The backwoodsman could be identified as a typically American figure, but in him there was also discernible the earlier character of the Yankee. Neither alone seemed capable of sustaining the weight of national consciousness, but the "two figures semed to join in a new national mythology, forming a striking composite, with a blank mask in common, a similar habit of sporting in public the faults with which they were charged, both speaking in copious monologues, both possessing a bent toward the self-conscious and theatrical, not merely because they appeared on the stage but because of essential combinations in mythical character" (*American Humor,* p. 67).

The third major figure whose character became permanently etched into the emerging portrait of the American was the Negro. Other ethnic types had appeared briefly and though some were destined to persist on the stage (the Dutchman and the immigrant Irishman, for example) none exerted so strong a hold on the popular imagination —and this despite his slave status. The attempt to determine the relationship of black culture to our national life has permeated every field of American scholarship. Sociologists, political scientists, historians, musicologists, and literary critics have juggled the issues concerning the Negro's special status in our society. They are far from being decided, as contemporary agitation throughout the country reveals; but even when the discussion has been heated by special pleadings or obscured by deeprooted prejudices, the result has always been a clarification of our national aspirations. It is as if, when we talk about the Negro, we inevitably uncover some basic truths about Americans as a whole. (As William Faulkner has shown us, to pursue the problem fully is to illuminate the condition of mankind.)

Constance Rourke began her discussion with a description of the vogue of minstrelsy, a subject which at the time was almost entirely unexplored.[8] Here again her province was popular rather than folk art, for the white minstrels filtered black traditions through their own consciousness, presenting to an incredibly large theater audience here and abroad a caricature of the plantation Negro. Precisely because of this stereotyped view of the Negro, the subject of minstrelsy has been a touchy one; the irony was difficult to see through the emotionally charged figures in blackface imitating the speech, movement, and above all the music and song of an oppressed and outcast people.

Miss Rourke was sharply aware of the popular response to minstrel tradition. "Blackface minstrelsy has long been considered a travesty," she pointed out, "in which the Negro was only a comic medium. To the primitive comic sense, to be black is to be funny, and many minstrels made the most of the simple circumstance. This exploitation was deeply resented by the anti-slavery leaders of an early day, and in the end they went far toward creating the idea that the Negro lacked humor" (*American Humor,* p. 74). Because of this distortion by the minstrels, the Negro's friends "collected and discussed and displayed only his religious pieces, the spirituals which have seemed his special creation."

Miss Rourke saw in the phenomenon of minstrelsy a major source of several important elements which added to the still unfinished portrait of the American. The first was a satirical humor that often blossomed into full-scale burlesque. White minstrels, including Dan Emmett, the most famous of them all, clearly borrowed fables and tunes from black tradition; but even when their intention was to glorify the plantation South the minstrels provided a strange and exotic effect which gave their caricatures a wider meaning. Negro folklore abounded in animal fables and nonsense songs that introduced a "bolder comic quality" than had been expressed in earlier American humor. But Miss Rourke identified in black tradition something more than a simple primitivism. Beneath the careless and often preposterous humor there was a tragic substratum which filled a gap in the configuration of American traits. The Negro had known defeat and it "could be heard in the occasional minor key and smothered satire" of his music and song. Like the earlier prototypes of the American, the Negro wore a mask, but unlike them his conscious satire was rooted in a vision of the human condition which the flourishes of his fantasy never obscured. That sense of the limitation and ultimate defeat of man which might have been the contribution of Calvinism to the American character, Miss Rourke's argument suggests, came rather through the experience of the Negro, though blunted and refracted for the popular mind by white minstrelsy. Indirectly though forcefully, a third figure was added to the Yankee and the Backwoodsman, merging like the earlier ones into the generic type.

White minstrelsy was a "double mask" which seemed to arouse "an instinctive response" among American audiences. We shall see, when we turn to the work of folklorists John and Alan Lomax, the germinal power of black folksong in the development of a native folk tradition in the United States. (Quite independently of Miss Rourke's research, the Lomaxes developed a similar view of the sources of an

American folksong tradition, emphasizing the gradual but unmistakable mixing of Afro-American and British folk motifs in a deceptively unself-conscious amalgamation.) Miss Rourke's formulation brought into sharp relief the deep imprint of black styles on popular rather than folk tradition, and it is an impact still discernible in our most recent experiences. Minstrelsy lasted long after the Civil War and the vogue of the blackface comedian persisted even longer. Periodically, however, black folk styles have penetrated popular song traditions and reached vast audiences: after minstrelsy there was the development of several varieties of jazz, from the distinctly black New Orleans style to the more widely dispersed white imitation which became known as "Dixieland"; in the period after the Second World War there emerged the highly popular vogue of "rock and roll," which was itself a commercialized version of "rhythm and blues"; then as a result of the revival of interest in American folksong there was the wide influence of a group of traditional black singers and instrumentalists, among them Huddie Ledbetter (Leadbelly). And most recently, as we shall see in some detail, the emergence of "rock" provides evidence of a similar movement. In all these cases the ultimate source of influence is black, but its main force flows through white performers and is received by white audiences. However masked and indirect this influence is, Miss Rourke was accurate in her assertion that it was widespread and persistent. And despite the generally flippant tone of the surface, there was always the tragic undercurrent: "The young American Narcissus had looked at himself in the narrow rocky pools of New England and by the waters of the Mississippi; he also gazed long at a darker image" (*American Humor*, p. 90). It was an image, we can say now with the perspective of forty years, that has sharpened and intensified rather than blurring and diffusing out of the picture of American life.

The first part of *American Humor* was an attempt to discover the sources of the American character by examining the underlying folk tradition which, as Herder had proposed, would reveal its authentic forms. After establishing her triptych Miss Rourke turned to environmental and institutional forces which helped to shape the larger patterns of American literature. Her central concern was with the influence of the frontier on native theater and religion.

Each of the three character types had strong associations with theater, a term which Miss Rourke opposed to the drama. The theatrical, she pointed out, "is full of experiment, finding its way to audiences by their quick responses and rejections. On the stage the shimmer and glow, the minor appurtenances, the jokes and dances and songs, the stretching and changes of plots, are arranged and altered almost literally by the audience or in their close company; its measure is human, not literary" (*American Humor,* p. 93). The last phrase contains the major insight, for it helps to explain the curious resistance in American literature to the classical and neo-classical conception of the sublime. As she noted later in connection with our novelists and poets, the movement is away from traditional forms which emphasize a high style and the hegemony of tragedy. The center of gravity was comic and as in earlier experiences it was a levelling agent with marked antagonism toward "highbrow" traditions. The theater is an especially sensitive gauge of this tendency. It "took a place which in a civilization of slower and quieter growth might have been occupied almost altogether by casual song and story; even the comic tale was theatrically contrived, with the teller always the actor, and the effect dependent upon manner and gesture and stress of speech" (*American Humor,* p. 93). No drama in the literary sense emerged from the nineteenth-century American theater, yet the theatrical was a native mode and, especially in the West, it "was a composite of native feeling."

The folklore of the American theater on the frontier is rich in clues to the main lines of American literary development in general. Miss Rourke's recitation of characteristic stories emphasizes the peculiar combination of pure romanticism superimposed on naive sensibilities. "On a small stage in a Kentucky village a gambler's family was pictured as starving," she recounts, "and a countryman rose from one of the boxes. 'I propose we make up something for this woman,' he said." During a Georgia production of *Pizarro,* twenty-four real Indians were employed as spearcarriers: "When the high priest, followed by the priests and virgins, began the invocations, the Creeks responded with a low, mournful humming sound which speedily took on threatening undertones and rose to a war song. When the chorus began to sing the Creeks broke into a war dance in which the King and Rolla were constrained to join until the sweat poured off their bodies, while the virgins dashed from the stage and locked themselves in their dressing rooms" (*American Humor,* p. 101). It is hard to know whether the tales are true or not, but they are in themselves a good example of American humor, one of whose functions is to pierce the façade of romanticism, emitting in the process a force and vitality which shatters the pretensions of mannered art. (This is precisely what the "redskin" is understood to have accomplished, even by his severest critics.) Yet though the tradition was founded on low humor, it is by no means uncomplicated. Like its forerunners, this genre was steeped in *double-entendre* and conscious satire. The major theme of these stage writers "was the false romanticism of American sentiment for the Indian." Their favorite form was the burlesque with its inevitable edge of satire. Fantasy, in their hands, became a source of lethal ridicule with a subject matter that ranged from obvious barbs in the direction of Longfellow to burlesques on the theories of free love, feminism, or political scandals. These were native themes and the mode of representing them led toward an essentially comic art which helps to define not only Mark Twain (who drew heavily and consciously upon these motifs) but such makers of the modern theater as Tennessee Williams. "This lawless satire" of the thirties and forties "was engaged in a pursuit which had occupied comedy in the native vein elsewhere. . . . Comedy was conspiring toward the removal of all alien traditions, out of delight in pure destruction or as a preparation for new growth" (*American Humor,* p. 110).

Miss Rourke did not make this frontier hypothesis in an articulate formulation, but it is so close to the main lines of Turnerian speculation that it merits attention. Over and over again the frontier has been defined by important critics and writers as the area in which the legacy of the Old World was wiped clean and the meaning of America written afresh. For Constance Rourke it was comedy which purged the old traditions and provided the basis for the new. As in the classical formulation by Frederick Jackson Turner, it was a process by stages through repeated contact with an unsophisticated but vital frontier existence. But where Turner emphasized the pragmatic and anti-intellectual propensities of the frontiersman, Miss Rourke saw a new mythology springing from the depths of the American wilderness. The difference is perhaps that, as a historian, Turner was too often unaware that he had shifted his ground to typological or mythical approaches. Miss Rourke's approach was almost always folkloristic and she was consequently sensitive to categories of analysis which were only implied in Turner's formulation.

Thus her discussion of the frontier led directly to the consideration of the religious revivals which she identified "in a fundamental and not irreverent sense" as belonging to the theatrical developments of the same period. The frontiersmen were "of the race which produced the leaping, heel-cracking comic figures who proclaimed their identity with the lightning and the alligator. They joined in the orgiastic forest revivals on the Red River and Gaspar River, shouting and pleading to be bathed in the blood of the lamb, and bending, writhing, jerking, falling, barking, and creeping over the ground like the creatures of the wilderness" (*American Humor,* p. 111). This is a conception of the frontier distinct from Turner's though it follows his general line that, as Miss Rourke put it, the "restraining bonds were broken of that rigorous faith that seemed a solid American inheritance from the older civilizations." Frontier religion, however, submerged the individual in a communal passion that was expressed in fantasy and legend. Though traditions associated with the theater as well as with revivalism had foreign sources, they soon "took on a native extravagance." These were the conditions of America's childhood, "extended and spatially widened by the opening of wilderness after wilderness, the breaking down of frontier after frontier."

As I noted earlier, one of Constance Rourke's main tasks was to provide evidence of a rich source from which an American literary tradition could be seen to flow. By exploring both folk and popular developments she more than made the point. "Far from having no childhood," she could argue, "the American nation was having a prolonged childhood." What she had shown was that despite its lack of a feudal or antique past, America had its own period of primitive accumulation upon which, and in general accordance with Herderian theory, a formal art tradition could be built. All of its preparation, however, led American literature to a unique expression "derived from the life out of which it sprang." If its natural level was not the sublime, even its comedy demanded special definition. Quoting Meredith's declaration that the comic poet can be produced only in a "society of cultivated men and women," Miss Rourke described the emergence of American humor from an unsophisticated and barbaric people. "To know comedy," Meredith had insisted, "you must know the real world." But the main forms of America's comic spirit were in the realm of fantasy and legend, in the extravagance of folk speech and the unbridled satire of popular theater. Its function, moreover, was not related to the traditional comedy of manners, whose purpose is to assert for the audience the values of society. Rather it became (as indeed it had been from the beginning of our national existence) a lever for radical and sometimes destructive criticism, not unlike the currently popular "black humor." If America's comic fantasies "failed to exhibit subtlety, fineness, balance, they had created laughter and had served the ends of communication among a people unacquainted with themselves, strange to the land, unshaped as a nation; they had produced a shadowy social coherence" (*American Humor,* p. 129). Although its central function was to unify the heterogeneous elements of our experience, its technique was poetic, "keeping that archetypal largeness which inheres in the more elementary poetic forms, with the inevitable slide into figure and that compact turn with unspoken implications which is the essence of poetic expression."

Here the most valuable of Miss Rourke's critical observations comes into clearest focus. It is essentially a revision of Herderian theory which, on the one hand, avoids a mechanical application of the idea to American conditions and, on the other, helps to explain the distinct configurations of our native tradition. The materials brought together during our period of germination, she maintains, existed on several levels. Hence "this comic poetry could not be called folk-poetry, but it had the breadth and much of the spontaneous freedom of folk-poetry; in a rough sense its makers had been the nation. Full of experiment and improvisation, it did not belong to literature; but it used the primary stuffs of literature, the theater that lies behind the drama, the primitive religious ceremony that has been anterior to both, the tale that has preceded both the drama and the novel, the monologue that has been a rudimentary source for many forms" (*American Humor,* p. 129). The primary phase in America was never, in Herderian terms, purely folk but already a hybrid concatenation of folk and popular. Jane Harrison had suggested that every great period in art must have the same circumstances of "a new spirit seizing or appropriated by an old established order." But that dictum seemed inappropriate for an evaluation of American development where "the American had cut himself off from the older traditions; the natural heritage of England and the continent had been cast away so far as a gesture could accomplish this feat." Where the tendency persisted it was in the direction of romantic nostalgia for the Indian; but, as Miss Rourke had shown, that became quickly a source of burlesque and satire.

In a more traditionally Herderian vein, Miss Rourke agreed that the outlines of an American literature proceeded from this substratum. "Such preludes have existed for all literatures," she maintained, "in songs and primitive ballads and a folk theater and rude chronicles. Great writers have often drawn directly from these sources; . . . from them literature gains immensely; without them it can hardly be said to exist at all." Like most literatures, the productions of America are related to an "anterior popular lore that must for lack of a better word be called a folk-lore." But no direct relationships can be drawn from this set of circumstances, "no simple, orderly completion." Behind the formal accomplishments of our writers there lay the groundwork which had been fashioned by the Yankee, the Backwoodsman, and the Negro, as well as the "strollers of the theater and of the cults and revivals, the innumerable comic story-tellers and myth makers. . . ." The comic spirit had been lawless and irreverent, concerned with the generic image rather than close observation of the individual character or of "society." Indeed the American literary tradition veered always toward the "inner view, the inner fantasy, which belonged to the American comic sense. Genius necessarily made its own unaccountable revelations. Many external influences were at work. But the basic patterns, those flowing unconscious patterns of mind and feeling which create fundamental outlines in expression, had been developed in a native comic lore. The same character was at work on both levels" (*American Humor*, p. 132).

Constance Rourke stopped just short of making a major statement about the relationship of her analysis to the characteristic attitudes of American writers toward the idea of genre. It was possible, consequently, for Hyman to criticize her method for what he conceived to be a simple-minded manipulation of the relationships between folk and fine art traditions. It results, he argued, in a "certain distortion —Hawthorne becomes a teller of folk tales, *Moby Dick,* with its comic Biblical names and nautical puns, a cousin to the jokebooks of the day—but sometimes the distortion is a brilliant restoration, like the recognition of Lincoln as a literary figure."[9] The left-handed compliment, I submit, does little justice to the breadth or subtlety of Miss Rourke's accomplishments in *American Humor.* In the closing sections of the book she does provide a somewhat sketchy analysis of the main lines of our literary tradition which flow from the sources she was the first to identify as crucial to our literary development. But as I have tried to show, she does not conceive of our literary figures as "outgrowths of folk culture." To the contrary, her comment was that "though he drew upon traditional material, Hawthorne could not rest at ease as the great English poets have rested within the poetic tradition that came to them through the ballads and romances, or as the great English novelists have drawn upon rich local accumulations of character and lore" (*American Humor,* p. 151). What she could explain was Hawthorne's predilection for the "romance," which led him to transmute "regional legends into inner moods," or as in *The Scarlet Letter,* to slip into an "irreverent rude comedy far from the conscious Puritan habit." (Miss Rourke may have had in mind that truly humorous scene, redolent with hints of Elmer Gantry and other lecherous clerics, in which Dimmesdale, fresh from his forest encounter with Hester, almost seduces the most virginal of his parishioners.)

Constance Rourke's insights led her to an understanding of the constant attack by American writers on established canons of taste and style. And it is important to underscore the influence of Herder's thought on her work. Like Emerson and Whitman she went directly to the heart of his meaning, observing that "a mild nostalgia quickly took the place of Herder's bold creative concept of the folk as a living wellspring of poetry and song. This was brought about mainly through the selective work of Schlegel and the Grimms, whose explorations of folklore and folk-song had great value but who developed to an extreme the romantic concept of primitive or folk-life which had first been touched upon by Montaigne. Antiquarianism began to cast its long insidious spell, and inquiries as to the folk-arts came to be regarded as minor excursions into the petty or the quaint."[10] No criticism can ever completely contain either the sources or the effects of art, as no literature can finally fulfill its own expectations. But our debt to Constance Rourke stems from her awareness of the major strategy which Americans have utilized to establish their own sense of identity and coherence. Though it is an approach closely approximating Herder's, she noted the significant function of comedy as a way of blunting the criticism of European "high" cultures. Moreover, it makes us aware of the persistent use of the mask or persona as the characteristic response to foreign criticism. The barbarism of the American (who is easily tagged as the redskin) reveals itself to be a more complex state than many critics have perceived, partly because it is itself a literary strategy, partly because the folk sources from which it derives are more sophisticated than the palefaces have allowed themselves to recognize.

We can see the implications of this circumstance by looking closely at "The Arkansas Traveler," one of the most widely disseminated songs in American folk tradition. According to an early account, "The story . . . was founded on a little incident which occurred in the campaign of 1840" during a tour of the backwoods area of Arkansas by a Little Rock politician.[11] Since that time, the song has been in oral tradition, and it is one of those creations that has straddled folk and popular levels of culture through its adoption by minstrel players and professional singers. To the present day it is a standard part of the country music repertoire on radio, television, and recordings.

One reason for the song's continued popularity is its reflection of the tensions which still exist between rural and urban life in the United States. Country audiences respond enthusiastically to the dialogue between the Squatter and the Traveler, while citybred listeners are usually appalled by what they consider to be the corny humor of the piece. Like many folk materials, "The Arkansas Traveler" is a lot more complicated than it appears to be on the surface; there is a deeper significance that the urban-rural tension masks. But the difference in responses to the song by city and country audiences reflects the complexity of the strategy of humor it employs, and it is this strategy and its relationship to American humor that I want to discuss here.

Although a good many variations of the song exist, all of them develop from the same dramatic situation. A traveler who is lost in a backwoods area inquires from a squatter or farmer for directions which will get him home. The squatter is usually seated on his front porch playing the fiddle or picking a banjo. After each section of dialogue, the squatter plays the first part of the tune. (It has become so well known it is often used to introduce or identify rustic characters.) Some typical exchanges proceed as follows:

SQUATTER: Hello, Stranger.
TRAVELLER: Which one of those forks in the road do you take to town?
s: I don't know. I keep *my* forks up on the shelf. (*Here the* SQUATTER *plays the first part of the tune.*)
s: Hello Stranger.
T: Can you take this road to Grassville?
s: Can't see why you should. They got one there already.
T: Is that stream fordable?
s: Those ducks forded it this morning.

After several of these encounters, the traveler becomes aggressive and, instead of asking for information, begins to make nasty remarks about the squatter, his crops, and his family.

T: Your corn's mighty little and yellow.
s: Yup. I planted the yallah kind.
T: How many children have you got?
s: I don't know. Sal will roll a pumpkin under the bed, roust 'em out and count 'em.
T: What are your children all named?
s: They all named Sal; 'cept the little foolish 'un: his name's Sal, too.

In one version it is raining and the traveler says, "Your roof is leaking; why don't you fix it?"

s: How can I? It's raining too hard.
T: Then why don't you fix it when it stops raining?

s: Why should I? It don't leak then.
t: There ain't much difference between you and a fool, is there?
s: The only thing I see between you and me is a fiddle. [*Or,*
    "There's only my porch and a yard between us."]
t: You're not very smart, are you?
s: Nope. But then *I* ain't lost.

In another well-known version the Traveler asks the farmer why he
doesn't play the second part of the tune. The Squatter replies, "You
don't look much like a fiddler, but if you think you can play more
on to that tune, you're welcome to try." The Traveler does play the
other part, revealing that he is an accomplished country fiddler, after
which the Squatter invites him to stay the night and share the meager
provisions (and whiskey) of the household.

The tension between city and country life is the source of the
song's humor. The Traveler stands for the city and civilization, while
the Squatter represents the country and nature. The city slicker, lost
in the backwoods, is prepared for the silly answers he receives to his
questions. Indeed it is exactly what he expects from a "dumb farmer."
And, of course, this is precisely the attitude of city audiences toward
the humor of the song: taking it at face value, they find it corny,
because the Squatter is himself a "cornball"—a hick. The antagonism
between rural and urban folk is as old as the city mouse-country
mouse fables of antiquity. But the confrontation between the civilized
traveler and the barbaric squatter recalls again the Turnerian notion
that a distinctive American culture arose from the wilderness, which
is the major force that turned the civilized European into the native
American. Despite well-founded criticism of Turner's hypothesis, it
has been difficult to deny the deep-rooted sentiment that American
development proceeded by virtue of a series of contacts between
civilized outposts and "primitive settlements." The process began with
the first European plantations and continued across the continent from
East to West. At each point of contact, according to Turner, the impact
of the wilderness was felt by the Europeans until, by a gradual process
of attrition, they were stripped of their Old World characteristics. It
was this persistent struggle between East and West that Turner identified as the dynamic of American development, and it resulted in a
society from which European influences were eliminated. "The wilderness," he maintained, "masters the colonist. It finds him a European
in dress, industries, tools, modes of travel, and thought. It takes him
from the railroad car and puts him in the birch canoe. It strips off
the garments of civilization and arrays him in the hunting shirt and

moccasin. It puts him in the log cabin of the Cherokee and Iroquois and runs an Indian palisade around him. Before long he has gone to planting Indian corn and plowing with a sharp stick; he shouts the war cry and takes the scalp in orthodox Indian fashion."[12] Turner is quite serious about this assertion that a stage in the development of the American character is clearly the emergence of the redskin —the *peau rouge*. And he does not concern himself with the inference drawn from that position that indeed the American is always best defined as an Indian.

But for some time before Turner presented his now famous paper (in 1893) on the significance of the frontier in American history, the Indian provided one of the masks which the American character adopted in its confrontation with the Old World. (The Boston Tea Party, indeed, weds the notion to the earliest aspirations of American independence.) Later on, Southwestern humorists recognized the potential humorous strategy of this circumstance and developed it into a subtle literary approach. Utilizing what Walter Blair has called the framework technique, writers such as Augustus Baldwin Longstreet, Thomas Bangs Thorpe, and Johnson J. Hooper emphasized the incongruity between the civilized world on the one hand and the primitive society that developed in frontier areas of the South on the other.[13] A typical story would begin with a realistic description of the scene, couched in a highly literary diction. Then the author would introduce the storyteller himself, who would proceed to tell the tale in his own vernacular. It is this contrast between the literary style of the author and the vernacular of the storyteller that, according to Blair, accounts for the rich comic appeal of the Southwestern writers. The difference in levels of speech that the framework reveals also indicates a contrast in levels of culture—the narrator's diction represents urban (and generally Eastern) sophistication, while the storyteller's invokes an image of backwoods illiteracy. And these social distinctions were obvious to the Eastern audiences for whom the frontier humorists wrote.

"The Arkansas Traveler" exhibits a variation of the cultural conflict that the framework technique suggests. As the editors of the Arkansas volume in the American Guide Series attest, the characterization of the Squatter touched a sensitive spot in the nineteenth century as well as in our own time: "The vogue of the tune and dialogue spread even more widely when they were used in a play called *Kit, The Arkansas Traveler,* that delighted New York audiences of the 1880's. At the time, Arkansas people felt that the play was too full of pistol shots and bowie knives to be realistic. Even today many persons slightly resent the notion that the Squatter and his cabin were ever considered typical of the state."[14] The comment suggests, however, that the editors of the volume missed the nature of the humor. The Squatter knows that the Traveler considers him a backwoods barbarian. The strategy of the humor, consequently, is based on the Squatter's willingness to act the role of an ignorant rustic, thus taking advantage of the traveler's gullibility as well as his prejudices. The series of puns and corny jokes is only humorous if the listener knows the farmer is turning the tables on his adversary; the backwoodsman adopts a pose of innocence and naiveté that reverses the roles, making the city slicker the butt of the joke. In short the humor derives from the Squatter's ability to puncture the condescension and snobbery of the Traveler at the very time that the latter is looking down his nose at the "bumpkin." The range of sensitive areas that "The Arkansas Traveler" can cover is one of its major attributes. The Squatter defends his intelligence, his abilities as a farmer and a parent, and even his artistry as a fiddler. In one encounter the Squatter's wife, Sal, comes to the door. After a few preliminary questions which indicate his lack of respect for the intelligence of backwoods women, the Traveler asks: "Any Presbyterians around here?" Sal responds: "There's one right up there on the wall; my husband skins everything he shoots." Here the Traveler invokes the prestige of what for the frontier is a "high church" and Sal's comment only confirms his opinion of the barbarousness of backwoods religion. (The Squatter and his wife are probably Methodists or, even worse, Baptists.) But the humor comes again from the ability of the country folk to exploit the city slicker's gullibility and pomposity.

In his essay, "How to Tell a Story," Mark Twain insisted that the humorous strategy I have been discussing is uniquely American. The teller of the typically American humorous tale, he says, proceeds in a rambling and disjointed way, but "the listener must be alert," for the storyteller will often spring the joke "in a carefully casual and indifferent way, with the pretence that he does not know it is a nub." Describing a story told by James Whitcomb Riley "in the character of a dull-witted old farmer," Twain noted: "The simplicity and innocence and unconsciousness of the old farmer are perfectly simulated, and the result is a performance which is thoroughly charming and delicious. . . . To string incongruities and absurdities together in a wandering and sometimes purposeless way, and seem innocently unaware they are absurdities, is the basis of the American art, if my position is correct."[15] The mask of innocence and the dead-pan delivery that Twain described as uniquely American are not limited to the

Southwestern humor from which Twain developed. The Down East humorists employed it too, in the character of the Yankee, who was also a rustic. And as Blair has pointed out, the framework technique itself was well known in European fiction, in the works of Boccaccio, Chaucer, and others. But there is a sense in which Twain's comment is an accurate and perceptive insight into the strategy of American humor, for underlying the tension between the city slicker and the country bumpkin is a conflict that is indeed peculiarly American. It comes into focus if we recall the deep-rooted conception of many Europeans that America was a wilderness inhabited by uncivilized backwoodsmen. If for some the New World was a garden, its tillers were nonetheless seen to be simpleminded farmers, untouched by the cultural advantages of European civilization. Because of its youth and its remoteness from the centers of high culture, America was, in this view, occasionally enticing but patently inferior to the Old World. In response to this identification, the American has consistently faced his European antagonists with a show of bravado. But he has as often relied on just the kind of dissembling which "The Arkansas Traveler" depicts. In fact, if one enlarges the scope of the antagonism between the Squatter and the Traveler, he perceives the outline of a more basic conflict. The Traveler is not only a city dweller, but an east-erner who, in his point of view toward the backwoodsman, shows himself to be a European. The Squatter, on the other hand, is not merely a farmer or rustic; he takes on the characteristics of the aboriginal American as well. From earliest times, the European (Mar-tineau, De Tocqueville, or Dickens) has actually encountered the dissimulating American. The strategy of humor "The Arkansas Trav-eler" employs is uniquely American because it is based on the theme of cultural conflict between the European and the American, and as Constance Rourke has pointed out, the international theme was cen-tral to our culture from the very beginning. The Traveler-Squatter antagonism, which seems to be regional, masks a deeper tension between the European traveler, who is smug and condescending, and the American native, who cleverly reverses the roles. He is that bar-barian whose vitality and poetic expression Emerson and Whitman so admired, and his essential defense against gentility is a trenchant humor.

At various points in his career Mark Twain invoked the situation as well as the strategy of "The Arkansas Traveler." His first pub-lished sketch was called "The Dandy Frightening the Squatter." It is a very short description of an encounter between a squatter and a "spruce young dandy" who attempts to impress his lady companions by insulting a backwoodsman.[16] The matter is settled very quickly: "The squatter calmly surveyed him a moment, and then, drawing back a step, he planted his huge fist directly between the eyes of his astonished antagonist, who, in a moment, was floundering in the turbid waters of the Mississippi." The physical struggle overshadows the more sophisticated cultural conflict that Twain emphasized in later works, but the sketch indicates his familiarity with the motif.

The basis for the humor of much of *Roughing It* (1872) comes from the exposure of easterners to the society of western roughnecks and barbarians. The famous encounter between the preacher from an eastern seminary and the Nevada silver miner, Scotty Briggs, derives its comic appeal from the fact that the minister interprets Scotty's metaphors literally; like the Traveler, the preacher is already confirmed in his impression of the depths of depravity and savage behavior that Scotty's vernacular suggests. In *Life on the Mississippi* (1883), Twain poses as a New Englander in order to trap a river pilot into spinning tall tales. This is what might be called the "double reverse" variation of the theme for, like the analogous version of "The Arkansas Traveler," the Traveler is really a Squatter in disguise. Thus in the chapter entitled, "My Incognito Is Exploded," the river pilot tells the outrageous story of the alligator reefs with the full knowledge of his visitor's identity. At the conclusion of the scene, Twain "plays the second half of the tune": "Here . . . you take her and lie a while," the pilot says, "—you're handier at it than I am: Trying to play yourself for a stranger and an innocent! Why, I knew you before you had spoken seven words . . . Now take the wheel and finish the watch; and next time play fair, and you won't have to work your passage."

In *The Innocents Abroad,* which was published in book form in 1869, Twain exposed the deepest level of the cultural conflict implicit in "The Arkansas Traveler." Section Twenty-seven contains the famous scene between the American pilgrims and their Italian guide, whom they have named Ferguson because they cannot pronounce his real name. This time the American is the Traveler; but the sea change has not altered the technique of humor. The narrator explains that he has had quite enough discussion of Michael Angelo's universal genius. "I used to worship the mighty genius of Michael Angelo," he says, but "I do not want Michael Angelo for breakfast—for luncheon—for dinner—for tea—for supper—for between meals." In order to get even with Ferguson, the Americans "played that game which has vanquished so many guides for us— imbecility and idiotic questions. These creatures never suspect—they have no idea of a sarcasm." The resulting dialogue is humorous if one understands that behind the mask of literalism and naive responses is the figure of the Squatter, who knows full well that the Traveler thinks he is stupid. But here one part of the mask is off: the confrontation is clearly between the uncultured American and the sophisticated European. The doctor is chosen for the lead role, the narrator says, because "he can keep his countenance and look more like an inspired idiot and throw more imbecility into the tone of his voice than any man who lives. It comes natural to him." The nature of the conflict is underscored by the fact that "guides in Genoa are delighted to secure an American party, because Americans so much wonder and deal so much in sentiment and emotion before any relic of Columbus." The pressure to pay homage to Columbus only emphasizes what the narrator has felt all along in his relationship with the guide: America was, after all, discovered by Europeans and one expects the aborigine to acknowledge his spiritual fathers. The doctor, however, will have none of it, and like the archetypal American of "The Arkansas Traveler" dialogue, he outrages the Italian guide by assuming a mask of ignorance which the latter accepts as reality.

Presented with a manuscript bearing the signature of Columbus, the doctor pretends not to recognize the name. Then he criticizes the penmanship, emphasizing the superiority of his own countrymen: "Why, I have seen boys in America only fourteen years old that could write better than that." On being shown a bust of Columbus, he again pretends to be unfamiliar with the name or the accomplishments of the subject. "Well, what did *he* do?" the doctor asks. When informed that Columbus discovered America, he replies authoritatively: "Discover America. No that statement will hardly wash. We are just from America ourselves. We heard nothing about it." For good measure the doctor identifies himself as a true barbarian by pretending that he cannot distinguish between the bust and the pedestal. The narrator adds, "That joke was lost on the foreigner—guides cannot master the subtleties of the American joke." The final incident in the scene caps the American's disavowal of his European heritage with a show of disrespect for antiquity and the cradle of civilization itself. The last trump in the guide's hand is an Egyptian mummy that the narrator acknowledges to be "the best preserved in the world, perhaps." But the doctor continues as before:

"Ah,—Ferguson—what did I understand you to say the gentleman's name was?"

"Name?—he got no name!—Mummy!—'Gyptian mummy!"

"Yes, yes. Born here?"

"No! *'Gyptian* mummy!"

"Ah, just so. Frenchman, I presume?"

"No!—*not* Frenchman, Not Roman!—born in Egypta!"

"Born in Egypta. Never heard of Egypta before. Foreign locality, likely. Mummy—mummy. How calm he is—how self-possessed. Is, ah—is he dead?"

"Oh, *sacre bleu,* been dead three thousand year!"

The doctor turned on him savagely:—

"Here, now, what do you mean by such conduct as this! Playing us for Chinamen because we are strangers and trying to learn! Trying to impose your vile second-hand carcasses on *us!*—thunder and lightning, I've got a notion to—to—if you've got a nice *fresh* corpse, fetch him out!—or by George we'll brain you!"

Mark Twain's critical abilities have often been belittled by scholars who have cast him in the role of an intuitive but unsophisticated writer. But although he was capable of playing the Squatter to the hilt (in his writing as well as his life), more recent scholarship has gone far toward revealing that there is a good deal of insight and artistry beneath the surface of the pose. His use of "The Arkansas Traveler" motif signifies more than just another instance of Twain's reliance on materials from American folk tradition. It reveals as well his sensitivity to the thematic possibilities of the cultural conflict between Europe and America. For Twain, as for American writers since the beginning, the undercutting of the American stereotype by a character who played the expected role with a wily enthusiasm was indeed a basic strategy of humor.

It was a variation of this strategy that enabled Twain to achieve his greatest success artistically and ideologically. For in *Adventures of Huckleberry Finn* he removed the framework and committed himself to a full evocation of the national character in its own terms and its appropriate language. As Constance Rourke has pointed out, the traditional rendering of the American character involved a mask so complete that the deepest levels of feeling and experience remained secretive. On the one hand, this resulted in a movement toward mythical presentation and a reliance on fantastic elements not unlike folk tale or romance (in Hawthorne's sense of the term). But on the other, it left a nagging question which remained difficult to answer: suppose the mask were lifted and we discovered at the heart a literal barbarism. Perhaps, that is to say, the strategy I have been discussing is less a pose than a defense for a callowness even greater than unfriendly critics had always insisted upon. Twain's answer is supplied through indirection; one needed to look carefully to realize how closely he reproduced the urgings of Emerson, exposing just those seemingly barbarous materials upon which a distinctly American art could be based, investing them with a virtue hitherto reserved for the inhabitants of antiquity or the Old World. We recognize now that as much as Whitman's, Twain's was a language experiment which, at bottom, demonstrated that an American vernacular was capable of sustaining the full range of human experience in an expression consciously devoid of high diction. (Yet Twain is not literally a folk writer, though like Whitman he operates with a folk ideology similar to Herder's and Emerson's.) At the same time we can recognize in Huck the essential outlines of the Squatter, whose strategy Twain has translated into a sophisticated ironic tone which enabled him to control the ideological issues in the book. As Henry Nash Smith has pointed out,[17] it was Twain who first discovered the possibilities of a controlled point of view which enabled him to present a character's experience with a subtlety akin to James's, though it is the latter with whom the technique is associated. Again, as with Whitman, we can recognize that beneath the seemingly offhand surface which flaunts a casualness and disregard of form, there is a remarkably full demonstration of artistry and style which fulfills the requirements of an American prose. At least in *Huckleberry Finn,* Twain exposes an American voice only comparable to the accents of Whitman in poetry. It was a revelation of the national character, close to folk diction, in a basically humorous mode, with clear intimations of myth and diverging markedly from the pattern of the English novel. Its basic style has been well defined by Huck himself in his description of the widow's supper table: "When you got to the table you couldn't go right to eating, but you had to wait for the widow to tuck down her head and grumble a little over the victuals, though there warn't really anything the matter with them. That is, nothing only everything was cooked by itself. In a barrel of odds and ends it is different; things get mixed up, and the juice kind of swaps around and the things go better." I don't think that Twain made that statement as an analogy to his esthetic; but its point is relevant nevertheless. *Huckleberry Finn* exemplified just such an opposition to formal pieties which served the hypocritical aims of the genteel community. On the one hand, Huck is accurate in describing the prayer as a "grumble" which takes no cognizance of its meaning. On the other hand, the difference between everything being cooked by itself and the mish-mash that Huck prefers is not far from an esthetic commitment: the widow's cooking is formally correct, but sterile. The phrase that reminds us of Whitman is "and the juice kind of swaps around," which clearly identifies Huck as a culinary barbarian. And right to the moment of his moral crises Huck is willing to play the role; he is the Squatter to the last as he condemns himself to hell for making a decision which brings him to a deep faith in the spiritual community of men. Twain was willing for his hero to be identified as an American barbarian, the while undercutting his genteel critics, artistically and ideologically. But this should not allow us to forget that it is a studied position, a literary strategy which makes Santayana's comment inapplicable. In the light of Constance Rourke's approach we can see that the pose which so confounds some of Whitman's and Twain's critics is less an innovation than a calculated use of inherited materials. As in the case of James's American heroes and heroines, the surface barbarism only masks a sensitivity and honesty which puts to shame the affectations of their respectable antagonists. We miss this only if we take the strategy of humor at face value, thus reproducing just that error which the Traveler makes in his estimate of the Squatter. Still, and for reasons that will occupy us next, the strategy works all too well.

Chapter Five
The Sources of American Folksong

CONSTANCE ROURKE'S attempt to define the American character in terms of the folklore created in this country was a major and pioneering effort. But it was a theoretical construct which offered only passing evidence of the actual folk traditions with which she dealt. Moreover, in her concern with all the fields of folk activity (she included folk art and design as well) she could provide only an inkling of what had been created here in folksong and folk music. Folksong was an especially critical area, for the area of song had the greatest appeal to early collectors who identified it as the oldest as well as the most impressive of folk creations. Folklore means essentially oral, narrative styles, and while it is of the highest significance it lacks the appeal of an art which weds music and song (and sometimes dance) in a form that can be readily compared with the accomplishments of ancient bards and their traditions. As early as Herder's speculations, it had been emphasized that the deepest levels of a people's culture are revealed by their national songs, and in the absence of clear evidence that such a tradition existed in this country it was still possible to insist on the inferiority of America's cultural heritage. Hence it is necessary to examine closely the response of critics to American folksong and folk music, and especially the work of John and Alan Lomax. Their views follow the major lines of the Emerson-Whitman tradition which, as I have shown, leaned heavily on the ideas of Herder. Again the matter of influences is less important than the fact that, finding themselves in a position similar to that of Emerson and Whitman, the Lomaxes responded to assertions of America's cultural inferiority with similar arguments. The position of the Lomaxes with regard to the nature and meaning of an American folksong tradition, the relationship between folksong and national culture, and above all the affirmation of democratic principles provides an insight into the continuity of American thought from the nineteenth century to the present time.

But in order to understand the Lomaxes' attempt to define the nature of an American folksong tradition, we need to keep in mind the approaches of earlier critics and scholars. These were informed by two main conceptions which we have already encountered in the general response to the possibilities of an American cultural development.

The first is that there simply isn't any American folksong. As Gilbert Chase has pointed out, the earliest comprehensive history of music in America was written by an Alsatian musician who visited the United States in 1856 and commented that "the people's song is not to be found among the American people. . . . From the hearts of such people, in whose eyes an innocent smile, a merry laugh, was considered a sin, no naive, cheerful, sweet melody could spring. His [the American colonist's] emotional life was stifled and repressed: therefore there are no folk poetry and no folk-songs in America."[1] This argument is based on the erroneous idea that Puritanism was inimical to musical expression, but it is only one of numerous explanations for the apparent lack of folksongs in America. As late as 1904, Chase points out, a historian of American music devoted sixteen out of 423 pages to a discussion of American folk music, explaining, "It must be admitted that in this field America is rather barren." In one sense, this is an inversion of the Herderian theories we have considered earlier. America has no national literature, hence, there must obviously be lacking an anterior folk tradition from which it could have developed. Given the wide acceptance of the first assumption, the second logically follows. A more important argument is closely related to the approach taken to our literature by a good many critics, namely that any folksong found here would be simply a reflection of European, especially British, traditions. This latter view is still widely held and is manifested in terms of what may be called the ballad hierarchy— the idea that the ballad is the most significant type of folksong. The persistent emphasis on ballad study by American folklorists indicates the prevalence of the view that folksong is essentially literature (or subliterature) rather than a genre in its own right, consisting of music as well as text; at the same time it reveals the subservience to a British ballad tradition, in relation to which American versions are identified as inferior and often "corrupt." Conscious affirmation of these views varies from critic to critic, but they represent, nonetheless, the main line of folksong criticism in the past fifty years; and taken together they have been the main stumbling blocks in the attempt to identify the nature of an American folksong tradition.

The hegemony of the ballad was securely established through the publication of Francis James Child's collection (1882–1898). Though a Bostonian by birth, Child's preoccupation with the study of British balladry had the effect of limiting severely the study of American folksongs. Like Percy and other early collectors he was mainly concerned with texts and through his influence at Harvard it was Child who, more by example than instruction, determined the course of collecting in America for the first several decades of the twentieth century. The impact of *The English and Scottish Popular Ballads* can hardly be overestimated. It represented the most painstaking research, classification, analysis, collection of texts, and became a model for the use of the comparative method of folklore investigation. But Child's influence had other less beneficent effects on collectors of folksong in Europe and America, for almost singlehandedly he established the ballad as the highest form of folksong and the only species worthy of intensive research. Moreover, his use of the definite article in the title of his work implied that all the important ballads had been collected and that anything else which turned up was of subsidiary value. In America the reliance on Child's authority prevented scholars from acknowledging the existence even of native balladry. Indeed it has only been recently that scholars have had the temerity to challenge the scope and the method of the Child canon. In his collection of American ballads, for example, G. Malcolm Laws has observed: "That Professor Child's collection contains the finest of British traditional ballads no one denies, but in it he neither defined the ballad nor fully explained his method of deciding what to include. It is becoming increasingly apparent that subjective considerations must have influenced his inclusion of some pieces and his rejection of others." Laws added, "It is vital for the purpose of this study to realize that British balladry does not begin and end with *The English and Scottish Popular Ballads.*"[2] The fact that criticism of Child was so late in coming underscores not merely the force of his remarkable scholarship; it indicates as well the deep feelings of American indebtedness to British culture. Child's work seemed to offer overwhelming evidence that American balladry was but a pale reflection of the British ballad tradition, and it was this view that prevented American scholars from perceiving the diversity and vitality of American folksongs.

The inadequacies of Child's approach had not been properly evaluated because he died before the last part of his work was published and before he had completed an essay which would have summarized the theoretical implications of his great work. Lacking such a definitive statement from the master, it became difficult to put one's finger on the nature of disagreements, and Child's authority was literally canonized. As Bertrand Bronson has pointed out: "It is very noticeable that of late recent students are becoming increasingly restive under Child's authority, more and more unwilling to grant a mere second-class citizenship to the ballads in their own collections which missed of his royal accolade."[3] According to Bronson, the "canon of the exclusively popular is not to be found in Child's collection and neither, by the same token, could it ever have existed in his mind as other than an abstract concept. Actually it was a fiction invented by the awe of his disciples and falsely equated with his collection as he left it." Bronson suggests that a peculiar combination of romanticism and Darwinism is responsible for the undue idolatry accorded to Child and his collection: "The ballad was, it was felt, a *genre* that had arisen, flourished, and declined in response to historic conditions that would not be repeated. Child, gifted with miraculous organ, had been able to discover all the extant examples and traces of this now all-but-extinct phenomenon and bequeathed the collection to posterity as a definitive record, adorned and illustrated by the light of his supreme knowledge. The reception of it as inviolable and entire was easy and natural to those who had worked day after day in the personal inspiration of his omniscient presence."[4]

The full codification of Child's theories about the ballad, however, came not from the master, but from his disciples, especially George Lyman Kittredge, who finished the work of editing the final part of the *Ballads*. In his introduction to the one-volume edition Kittredge wrote: "History as we understand it, is the written record or even the printed volume; it is no longer the accumulated fund of tribal memories, handed down by father to son by oral tradition. Yet everybody knows that, quite apart from what we call literature, there is a great mass of miscellaneous song and story which circulates among those who have neither books nor newspapers. To this oral literature, as the French call it, education is no friend. Culture destroys it, sometimes with amazing rapidity. When a nation learns to read, it begins to disregard its traditional tales; it feels a little ashamed of them; and finally it loses both the will and the power to transmit them. . . . To this oral literature belong the popular ballads and we are justified, therefore, in calling them 'folk poetry.' . . . As civilization advanced they were banished from polite society, but they lived on among the humble, among shepherds and ploughboys, and 'the spinners and the knitters in the sun,' until even these became too sophisticated to care for them and they were heard no more."[5] Kittredge's approach reveals the extent to which Herder's ideas were revised and romanticized. There is first of all a Rousseauvian nostalgia for the innocence of illiteracy. It suggests a relief from the complications of civilization and the problems inherent in the level of social life which literacy represents. What the civilized man lacks is exemplified by the simple life of the folk and the unsophisticated art which they produce. Since the bearers of folksong have usually been peasants and country folk, Kittredge writes with a marked agrarian bias. In addition to the traditional virtues accorded to agrarian life (self-reliance, physical and psychological health, and general vigor), Kittredge assumes the existence of a natural ability for the creation of folk art. And he insists that this ability cannot be imitated by civilized men. But whereas Herder postulated the force of folk tradition as a means of replenishing the artistic wells of sophisticated culture. Kittredge declares the channels of such interaction permanently closed. Thus Kittredge did not merely idealize the folk; he also affirmed the notion that when folk society comes into contact with "Culture" it is inevitably destroyed. The idea achieved the status of a given theorem whose main source was the authority of Child and Kittredge, though its validity had never been demonstrated. Indeed it was precisely this view that the Lomaxes called into question. But when Kittredge wrote his essay in the early 1900's there was no doubt in his mind that folk art was impossible within the confines of civilized society. Although his argument was essentially impressionistic it was forceful: civilization is "ashamed" of its traditional arts; the ballads are "banished" from polite society; at last, even the humble folk become sophisticated and Kittredge declares: "Ballad-making, as far as the English-speaking nations are concerned, is a lost art; and the same may be said of ballad-singing."[6]

Twentieth-century scholarship has emphasized the ballad to such an extent that critical accounts devote their main energies to unravelling the arguments of communalists, individualists, and followers (or opponents) of Child. D. K. Wilgus devotes half of his study to what he calls the "ballad wars," maintaining that such a procedure is demanded by the central tradition of folksong scholarship.[7] He has described in detail the points of view of such ballad critics as Gummere, Lang, and others who reflect the influence of Child as well as of German romanticism, and although I am not concerned with the specific arguments of these early ballad collectors, it is significant to note that, whatever the internal disagreements may have been, there was no essential questioning of the hierarchy of ballad study. As Wilgus points out, when the reaction by younger critics against the "armchair" collectors set in, it was argued that some of the ballads collected in the United States conceivably might have originated here. Such collectors as William Wells Newell, Phillips Barry, and Henry M. Belden may be seen as calling into question the Child canon; but it is important to emphasize the fact that their revolt took place within the framework of balladry. And despite the fact that some scholars attempted to relate the ballads to musical traditions, for the most part the folklorists continued to emphasize the literary significance of ballad poetry. Not until the valuable work of Bertrand Bronson was there any attempt to study the tunes associated with the Child ballads, despite the accuracy of Bronson's statement that "ballads without tunes are as unfulfilled, as paradoxical, as songs without words." The typical collection of American folksongs consisted of ballad texts with headnotes that explained their relationship to the Child canon. The collections were an attempt to provide a regional mapping of Child ballads (or variants) in America.

I should emphasize at this point that the scholarship centering around Child and the ballad is not in itself pernicious. The general idea of tracing the lines of cultural interaction among the nations of Europe and their influence in America is a noble one. Indeed much ballad scholarship has reflected elements of Herder's broadly humanitarian and internationalist conceptions. It is precisely this impulse which led Sigurd Hustvedt to explain: "A friend to whom I once spoke of the revival of folklore upon national sentiment objected that there is already too much of offensive nationalism in this poor world of ours. Let anyone who is similarly troubled in mind dismiss his fears. Folklore is at once national and international. No thoughtful student of folklore can possibly become a Chauvinist."[8] Nevertheless, the particular circumstances of American history and especially the idea of America as a young and inferior civilization, have diverted the humanistic tendencies inherent in folklore study. Far from elucidating the nature of folksong in America, balladry and the example of Child's scholarship were used to undercut the notion of a native folksong tradition. What Constance Rourke found to be a major view of American culture is reproduced precisely in the following comment by Stanley Edgar Hyman, which illustrates the perseverance of the ideas I have been describing. It emphasizes the hierarchy of the ballad, the idea that folksong is important mainly as a source of fine art poetry, and seeks to explain the basis for America's cultural inferiority: "What has happened to the Child Ballad in America, in sum, is that it has become inadequate narrative, aborted drama, happy-ending tragedy, corrupt meaningless verbiage, and bad poetry in general. Some of this may be the effect of transmission in time, which seems to degenerate and deteriorate folk literature wherever we can observe its effects. Some of it, however, is certainly the effect of the American ethos, with its denial of death, its resistance to the tragic experience, and deep repression of sexuality, its overriding pieties, and its frantic emphasis on the inconsequential and the optimistic. It almost seems that these ballad texts are bad precisely to the degree that they have become successfully American, that they reflect the dominant values and resemble other unlovely features of our popular culture."[9] In the context of folksong criticism in this country, Hyman's attitude is not in the least surprising. It is simply a more candid statement of what American folklorists have been saying since the beginning of the century. Even earlier, the journal dedicated to the collection and preservation of American folklore began with the following apology: "As respects old ballads . . . the prospects of obtaining much of value is not flattering. In the seventeenth century, the time for the composition of these had almost passed; and they had, in a measure, been superseded by inferior rhymes of literary origin, diffused by means of broadsides and songbooks, or by popular doggerels, which may be called ballads, but possess little poetic interest."[10] Almost seventy years later, Hyman argued against the pretense that American ballads "are high art when so many of them are patently trash."

At the annual meeting of the American Folklore Society in 1913, John A. Lomax, then retiring president of the organization, delivered an address entitled, "Some Types of American Folksong." He began with a reiteration of Kittredge's definition of the ballad as anonymous, communal, handed down by oral tradition; the ballads were a narrative in song, "the spontaneous poetic expression of the primitive emotions of a people. . . ." Lomax then posed the question, "Have we any American ballads?" "Let us frankly confess," he continued, "that, according to the definition of the best critics of the ballad, we have none at all." There is, however, a considerable stock of folksongs which we persist in calling ballads and which have similar sources and effects. The seven types of these so-called ballads he described as: (1) ballads of the miner; (2) ballads of the lumberman; (3) ballads of the inland (and mainly the Great Lakes) sailor; (4) ballads of the soldier; (5) ballads of the railroader; (6) ballads of the Negro; (7) ballads of the cowboy. He included as an additional category "songs of the down-and-out classes,—the outcast girl, the dope fiend, the convict, the jail-bird, and the tramp." His interest in these American songs, Lomax explained, was based on their importance as "human documents that reveal the mode of thinking, the character of life, the point of view, of the vigorous, redblooded, restless American, who could no more live contented shut in by four walls than could Beowulf and his clan, who sailed around the coasts of Norway and Sweden."[11] The principles expounded in this address formed the kernel of a system of ideas which were developed throughout the course of Lomax's long career as a collector, and extended by the work of his son, Alan. To be sure, Lomax's nomenclature was conditioned by the nature of his scholarly audience, which could only accept a discussion of folksong if it were framed in terms of the classical definition of the ballad. He admitted frankly, however, that American songs failed to conform to the accepted definition, and in practice he disregarded the proscription against placing serious value on anything but ballads. As we shall see, his use of the term ballad left him open to criticism (from such ballad scholars as Louise Pound and Cecil Sharp), but his identification of occupational groups, the Negro, the cowboy, and the outcast as the main source of American folksong materials was a major revision of the views accepted by the established canon. At a time when most scholars denied the existence (or the value) of an American folksong tradition outside the confines of Child variants, Lomax boldly identified the importance of a body of materials that existed in contemporary society. Although he clearly paid homage to Kittredge's general formulations, he did not accept the latter's dictum that balladry and ballad singers no longer flourished in the English-speaking world. Neither was he content to work within the well-established notion that folksong was valuable essentially as providing fodder for the creation of formal poetry. As his statement indicates, he viewed folksongs as a revelation of distinctly American modes of thought and life; like Herder in Germany, Lomax began to examine folksong as a means of discovering the nature of our national character. And though his conclusions were similar to those of Constance Rourke, Lomax was able to back up his arguments for an American tradition of folksong with an impressive number of recordings made in the field.

Lomax's early interest in folk materials is described in an autobiographical work, *Adventures of a Ballad Hunter* (1947). As a boy in Texas, Lomax had deep associations with Negroes, the country folk who took part in revival and camp meetings, and, most importantly for his later career, with the cowboy "knights" and their "toonaments." "During a period of twenty years," Lomax notes, "ten million cattle and a million horses were driven northward from Texas on the Chisholm Trail and other cattle trails. As the cowboys drove the cattle they sang and yodeled to them, they made up songs about trail life. I began to write down these songs when I was a small boy." After studying in a small agricultural college and the University of Texas, Lomax attended Harvard University where his early interest in cowboy songs was encouraged by Professor Barrett Wendell, who later introduced Lomax to Kittredge. With the help of these two men he secured a grant to collect "pioneer ballads," and with the aid of a succession of fellowships was able to publish in 1910, *Cowboy Songs and Frontier Ballads.* The little packet of songs Lomax collected as a boy became the model for the first serious study of folksong in America.

In his preface to the first edition, which also contained a congratulatory message from Theodore Roosevelt, Professor Wendell made it clear that he regarded the collection as a contribution to the understanding of folksong's relation to formal literature: "In this collection of American ballads, almost if not quite uniquely, it is possible to trace the precise manner in which songs and cycles of song—obviously analogous to those surviving from older and antique times— have come into being. The facts which are still available concerning the ballads of our own Southwest are such as should go far to prove or disprove, many of the theories advanced concerning the laws of literature as evinced in the ballads of the old world." What Lomax's book seemed to show about these theories, according to Wendell, was precisely what scholars had affirmed for many years. Here, inexplicably, was a sample of artless, unsophisticated yet vital poetry "like the sturdy roots from which the finer, though not always more lovely, flowers of polite literature have sprung." To compare these songs of Lomax's with "the immortalities of olden time is doubtless like comparing the literature of America with that of all Europe together." Yet they seemed "near enough beauty" to be commended to those "who care for the native poetry of America." Wendell's condescending comment about the relationship between Lomax's materials and the acknowledged masterliness of the Child ballads is easy to understand in view of the traditional attitude of academic scholars. Indeed it was as an example of rough folk poetry that most critics welcomed Lomax's book, and the fact that it contained no music seemed to underscore their approach. At this early stage, Lomax was not ready to argue, as he did later, that American folksong was the equal of any folk art, including the ballads in Child's collection.

But after paying homage to the scholarly tradition (the songs showed the survival of "the Anglo-Saxon ballad spirit that was active in the secluded districts of England and Scotland even after the coming of Tennyson and Browning"), Lomax emphasized in his introductory comments, "They are chiefly interesting to the present generation, however, because of the light they throw on the conditions of pioneer life, and more particularly because of the information they contain concerning the unique and romantic figure in modern civilization, the American cowboy." Lomax pointed out that the songs were created within the confines of the ranch community, "situated hundreds of miles from where the conventions of society were observed," where the men lived on "terms of practical equality." Therefore, even if a song started as an individual creation it soon became "the joint product of a number of them," expressing their common experiences, thoughts, and interests. The cowboy's isolation made him turn his back on the culture of the East, and his roving habits kept him on "the skirmish line of civilization," in an almost primitive state. This accounts for the pattern of profanity which pervades many of the songs which Lomax felt could not be printed "for general circulation." "To paraphrase slightly what Sidney Lanier said of Walt Whitman's poetry, they are raw collops slashed from the rump of Nature, and never mind the gristle. Likewise some of the strong adjectives and nouns have been softened,—Jonahed, as George Meredith would have said. There is, however, a Homeric quality about the cowboy's profanity and vulgarity that pleases rather than repulses. . . . He spoke out plainly the impulses of his heart. But as yet so-called polite society is not quite willing to hear." (Lomax continued to expurgate his materials, as most scholars had done since Percy, though he was candid enough to acknowledge it.)

As we follow Lomax's argument that the cowboy is a uniquely American figure, we can discern the outlines of yet another Turnerian interpretation of the frontier's role in shaping the American character. "Most cowboys," Lomax noted, ". . . were bold young spirits who emigrated to the West for the same reason that their ancestors had come across the seas. They loved roving; they loved freedom, they were pioneers by instinct; an impulse set their faces from the East, put the tang for roaming in their veins, and sent them ever, ever westward. . . . To the cowboy, more than to the goldseekers, more than to Uncle Sam's soldiers, is due the conquest of the West." The opposition of the cowboy to polite society, his contact with nature, and his position on the line between civilization and savagery were just those elements that Turner emphasized in his formulations. But Lomax's frontier hypothesis also allowed him to place the cowboy within the context established by Child and Kittredge, that is, as an unsophisticated child of nature in a primitive, communal culture. The frontier filled the role of a communal matrix from which balladry might emanate, just as the peasant communities of the middle ages provided the source for British balladry. At this point, Lomax was more anxious to satisfy the requirements of academic tradition than he was to develop the full implications of the frontier ideology, which would have led him (as indeed it did later) to basic disagreements with the ballad hierarchy itself. In the Cowboy Songs, therefore, Lomax was close enough to the position of Child to leave himself open to criticism in terms of the established criteria of folklore. And the criticism was not long in coming. The English musicologist, Cecil J. Sharp, who had published an impressive collection of British ballad survivals in the Southern Appalachians, sounded a familiar note. Comparing the survivals of British song which he found in the southern highlands with those that appeared in Lomax's collection, Sharp invoked the argument based on America's lack of a cultural past. The comparison between the mountain people and the cowboy, he noted, is a fair one "for the cowboys live a communal life almost as isolated and shut off from the world as that of the mountaineers, and feel, accordingly, the same compelling desire to express themselves in song. They are not . . . in any way inferior to their neighbors; they are, I take it, less illiterate, while the life they lead is more vivid and exciting and far richer in incident. Why then, is it that their songs compare so unfavorably with those of the mountain singers? It can only be because the cowboy has been despoiled of his inheritance of traditional song; he has nothing behind him. When, therefore, he feels the need of self-expression, having no inherited fund of poetic literature upon which to draw, no imaginative world into which to escape, he has only himself and his daily occupations to sing about, and that in a self-centered, self-conscious way, e.g., 'The cowboy's life is a dreadful life'; 'I'm a poor lonesome cowboy'; 'I'm a lonely bullwhacker'—and so forth."[12] Sharp was concerned mainly to discover what had been the fate of the ballads brought to this country by eighteenth-century English and Irish settlers. The mountain singer, he noted, "has come to create an imaginary world of his own and to people it with characters quite as wonderful . . . as the elfish creations of Spenser," because he built his songs on the traditional English heritage of poetry which he brought to this country. The cowboy, on the other hand, is truly American—he has no past to draw on and his poetry and music are predictably inferior. Had the cowboy actually produced a notable body of folksong it would have been remarkable, for he would have accomplished within his own community in a short time what had required centuries of evolution for the nations of the Old World.

The American folksong scholar, Louise Pound, criticized Lomax's collection on exactly opposite grounds, arguing that the cowboy had simply adapted Old World ballads to his own needs. In the first edition of *Cowboy Songs,* Lomax printed such songs as "The Cowboy's Lament," "Jesse James," "The Old Chisholm Trail," "Sweet Betsy from Pike," "Git Along Little Dogies," and many others which later became highly popular. Some of these were shown to be variants of

English or Irish ballads. Lomax himself had pointed out that many a cowboy was descended from Southern families and could therefore be expected to bring with him to the range songs well known in the rural South. ("The Cowboy's Lament," sometimes known as "The Streets of Laredo," was shown by Phillips Barry to be a variation of an eighteenth-century ballad, "The Unfortunate Rake." In the Irish version the hero is a soldier dying of venereal disease, rather than a cowboy who expires from a chest wound.) But not all of the *Cowboy Songs* were based on borrowed materials. Some had obviously arisen from the peculiar conditions of the cowboy's occupation, which demanded long trips on horseback or placed him on solitary vigils. The songs produced for such occasions were in no sense ballads, but rather personal, lyrical expressions. This is what Sharp criticizes when he notes that the cowboy's songs are "self-centered," for in the ballad as defined by Child and others the singer is "objective"—he does not comment personally on the action. Actually, traditional scholars insisted on this point because it seemed to buttress their argument that ballads were composed communally rather than individually. Hence as soon as a personal comment is noted, the ballad comes under suspicion of having been composed by one person and its folk character is lost. Nevertheless, Lomax insisted that there were elements of communal composition in the cowboy songs. Few songs could have expressed better the feelings of thousands of cowboys who travelled the long road called the Chisholm Trail than the rhymed couplets which were meant to be sung in the saddle and whose simple form allowed for easy improvisation. As cowboy after cowboy added to it, the song assumed epic proportions, Lomax observed, and he never was able to publish all the hundreds of verses he collected. Professor Pound's main concern was to refute Lomax's assertions that the cowboy ballads, like those of Child, were the result of communal composition. Her argument is that neither the Child Ballads nor the "good" cowboy songs could have been composed by unlettered people in the manner suggested by adherents of the idea of communal authorship. Of "The Old Chisholm Trail," for example, she says: "It is crude, without structure or clearly told story, is flat and vulgar in language, and is without striking or memorable quality." Miss Pound is willing to accept this song as indisputably of cowboy origin precisely to make the point that such "improvisations" are not "and never will be anything like a Child ballad, or anything like any other memorable ballad." Moreover she argues that those songs in Lomax's collection that have some merit are those for which some individual authorship can be established, and this helped her to substantiate the view that the best of the Child canon must also have been created by sophisticated poets, and only later passed down to the folk.

As an analogue of the ballad, the cowboy songs did indeed represent poor poetry, but as Lomax was to argue in his next collection, that is no criterion for their worth as folksongs. Louise Pound did not accept Kittredge's dictum that balladry was dead, nor did she deny the existence of an American folksong tradition. But she noted that "Already there are in America short narrative pieces, current over the countryside, lyric-epic in character, the authorship and the mode of origin of which are lost; and it is these, not the transient creations of cowboys or negroes, which form the real analogues for the English and Scottish popular ballads."[13] Because she accepted Child's notion of the aristocracy of the ballad among folksong types, it was inevitable that Professor Pound should have rejected just those materials upon which Lomax was to found his new canon of American folksong. According to what she considered the final test of the validity of any folksong—the possibility for its survival among the folk as a living creation—she predicted that the improvised productions of the cowboy and such Negro materials as "The Boll Weevil" (which was also included in *Cowboy Songs*) were "too crude, too structureless, too unoriginal, too lacking in striking or memorable qualities, to have much chance at survival."

The publication of *Cowboy Songs* was only the beginning of Lomax's attempt to reinterpret the tradition of American folksong. As I have noted, his early attempt to adjust his materials to the demands of ballad scholarship left him open to a variety of criticism. But as he continued to collect field recordings for the Library of Congress (in all he provided more than ten thousand recordings for the Archives of American Folk Song), he began to expand the ideas enunciated in his Folklore Society address. In collaboration with his son, Alan, Lomax published *American Ballads and Folk Songs* (1934) and, despite the retention of the term in the title, the book represents a forthright rejection of the ballad tradition in favor of the varied materials which he found to be characteristic of American folksong. The book announced the creation of a new canon of folksong for America, and its principles have been utilized by almost every succeeding editor of American folksong collections. The plan of organization was based on the categories first proposed in 1913, with special emphasis on the variety of Negro folksongs. There were railroad songs, Negro bad men, white desperadoes, southern mountain songs, blues, creole songs, reels, minstrel songs, play-parties, children's songs, vaquero and cowboy songs, mining, sailing, logging, canal and "overlanders" songs, white and Negro spirituals, as well as a category entitled, "whiskey and cocaine." This was a staggering inventory of song types and traditions and it was intended to deny the claim that America had no folk tradition of its own. At the same time it provided specific illustrations of the general argument which Constance Rourke had made only a few years earlier. In the introduction to the book, Alan Lomax observed, "Recently, a professor of music from Oxford University said in a public lecture at Bryn Mawr College: 'Since America has no peasant class, there are, of course, no American folksongs.' " Lomax denied that a peasant class was necessary for the production and propagation of folksong; yet it is significant that he found the richest materials among southern blacks, whose historic dependence on the land made them resemble a peasant group. The Negro was not, however, a peasant in the European sense of the word. Even during slavery there was a good deal of mingling of black and white musical culture, a phenomenon which was first noticed during the period of the Great Awakening, when blacks were welcomed to the camp meetings and revivals which swept through many parts of the South. George Pullen Jackson has noted that "the Negro found himself among real friends—among those who, by reason of their ethnic, social, and economic background, harbored a minimum of racial prejudice; among those whose religious practices came nearest to what he—by nature a religious person—could understand and participate in. He found himself a churchless pioneer among those white people who built meeting houses and invited him not only to attend their services and sing their songs, but also to join with them in full membership; white people who were concerned not only with his soul's welfare but also with his release from slavery."[14] There had even been Negro preachers before the American Revolution, men like Black Harry, "who during the revolutionary period accompanied Bishop Asbury as a drawing card and preached from the same platform with other founders of the Methodist Church."[15]

The significance of black folk styles in the development of American folk tradition is today generally accepted. But it should be recalled that most collectors rejected the notion that the Negro had contributed anything to American folksong, identifying his music as African and hence outside the main canon of our native tradition. Paradoxically, early historians developed the idea that since the Negro had been wrenched from his African environment and kept from full participation in this country, he became literally a man without a cultural or historical past.[16] In neither case could the music of the Negro be fitted into an American canon of folksong. Thus the founders of the American Folklore Society (among whom were Child and Kittredge) urged collectors to study black folk music because they were confident that such traditions would disappear in a short time. But the main stumbling block was that Negro songs were rarely ballads; on the one hand were spirituals, on the other a confusing variety of secular music, including blues, worksongs, dance tunes, and occupational songs. Collectors were in general agreement that the Negro's songs were either copied from white tradition or had no real connection with American developments.

In a manner similar to Constance Rourke's, Lomax began to identify black materials as central to an American tradition. The more Lomax continued to collect songs in the field, the more obvious were the connections and interactions between white and black traditions. When he became aware of the fact that educated Negroes were often loathe to sing for white collectors, Lomax hit on the idea of recording in the prison camps of the South. He explained that "In the prison camps . . . the conditions were practically ideal. Here the Negro prisoners were segregated, often guarded by Negro trusties, with no social or other contacts with whites, except for the occasional official relations. The convicts hear only the idiom of their own race. Many —often of greatest influence—were 'lifers' who had been confined in the penitentiary, a few as long as fifty years. They still sang the songs that they had brought into confinement, and these songs had been entirely in the keeping of the black man." Here, in what appeared on the surface to be a uniquely black culture, was an opportunity to analyze and explain the meaning of Negro folksong. The strong sense of the vitality of folksong in modern culture which animated the work of John and Alan Lomax, and which was bolstered by their contact with Negro folk music, led them to an ideological position which is closely related to the ideas of Emerson and Whitman. At the same time, the Lomaxes were, in effect, restating in American terms the implications of Herder's theories about folksong. As we follow the development of their theories we note the emergence of a democratic ideology which stressed the virtues of the common man and the dignity of oppressed groups such as the Negro, an emphasis on the functional character of folksong as a response to the particular experiences of American history, and finally an attempt to relate the significance of American folksong to its prototypes in the cultures of other nations. Already convinced that a substantial folksong existed here, the Lomaxes began to draw significant inferences about the nature and meaning of the national character which it reflected and the culture from which it emerged. As their collections of songs continued to be published they turned their attention to the issues which Herder, Emerson, and Whitman had already raised.

In the introduction to *Our Singing Country* (1941) earlier apologies for the dearth or inferiority of American songs were replaced by a full-throated declaration of musical independence. Our folk artists, the Lomaxes declared, "have created and preserved for America a heritage of folksongs and folk music equal to any in the world," and they took great pains to point out that few of these were ballads. Though there were obvious connections with the past, the new conditions in America were a source of a distinct and vital development: "These people have been wanderers, walking and riding alone into the wilderness, past the mountains and the broad rivers, down the railroad lines, down the highways. Like all wanderers, they have been lonely and unencumbered by respect for the conventions of life behind them. Remembering the old songs in their loneliness, throwing up their voices against prairie and forest track, along new rivers, they followed the instincts of their life in the new country. New songs grew up inconspicuously out of the humus of the old, thrusting out in new directions in small, but permanent fashion. There grew up a whole continent of people with their songs as much a part of their lives as their familiar ax, gun, or silver dollar. It took them long to recognize that new lives and new songs had been made here." The metaphor is organic: new life grows from the humus of the old, the songs thrusting out like leaves of grass. As Whitman had pointed out, America was a new experience which revived the ancient instincts of folk creation. Unlike academic folklorists who still tended to look for isolated, ethnic groups as a source of pure folk tradition, the Lomaxes enunciated a major principle in their assertion that the unique quality of American song is derived from the merging and hybridization of Old World stocks and styles: ". . . in mass, the songs are perhaps more unconventional than the new lives. The songs are a product of the mixing or extension of several peasant musical stocks—British, African, Spanish, French, and German. They are often repetitious; they are frequently trite and sententious; but taken all together, they reflect the life with more honest observation, with more penetrating wit and humor, with more genuine sentiment, and with more true, energetic passion than any other forms of American art, cultivated or subsidized." The fact that this reproduces almost precisely Whitman's earlier statement about the value of American folk humor is less important than the knowledge that both comments are based on the belief that the highest cultural values are to be found in the lowest orders of society—even among those most despised by genteel society. The songs in their volume, the Lomaxes pointed out, were collected not from manuscripts in libraries, but from active folksingers "who still sing the cowboy songs, the sea songs, the lumberjack songs, the bad-man ballads, and other songs that have no occupation or special group to keep them alive." Some of the best singers were a "Georgy cracker," a blind singer from the Ozarks, dispossessed Texas sharecroppers, farmers' wives, a tomato canning factory worker, a miner's wife who became a union organizer, a Vermont lumberjack now an automobile salesman, an Irish fisherman and Great Lakes sailor, a New England scissors grinder, a retired cowpuncher, and "dustbowl ballad-maker," Woody Guthrie. Essentially this was an argument against the antiquarianism of ballad hunters; at the same time, with the assistance of Ruth and Charles Seeger, the Lomaxes provided their readers with sensitive transcriptions of the tunes usually omitted from folksong collections. It was a catalogue worthy of *Leaves of Grass.* Finally the Lomaxes listed the names "of some of the singers who have moved us beyond all others that we have heard between Maine and New Mexico, Florida, and Michigan—the Negroes, who in our opinion have made the most important and original contributions to American folksong," among them "Aunt" Harriet McClintock, "Iron Head," "Dobie Red," Vera Hall, and Dock Reed. (Earlier the Lomaxes had uncovered the remarkable energies of Huddie Ledbetter, better known as Leadbelly. Their study of his life and art, *Negro Folk Songs as Sung by Lead Belly* [1936], was the first extended analysis of an American folksinger.)

In a conscious rejoinder to Sharp's criticism of the cowboy songs' lack of imagination or the absence in them of the "elfin creations of Spenser," the editors commented: "Nor does one find in them [American folksongs] an overwhelming desire to forget themselves and everything that reminds them of everyday life. The American singer has been concerned with themes close to his everyday experience, with the emotions of ordinary men and women who were fighting for freedom and for a living in a violent new world. His songs have been strongly rooted in his life and functioned there as enzymes to assist in the digestion of hardship, solitude, violence, hunger, and the honest comradeship of democracy." This was the fullest statement of the function of folksong in the development of American civilization. Just as Whitman viewed poetry as an agent for the evocation of democracy in America, so folksong was assigned the same function by the Lomaxes.

Folk Song U.S.A. (1947), the last work edited by Alan Lomax in collaboration with his father, is the clumination of their attempt to identify the nature of an American folksong tradition. It is the most important and influential collection of folksongs published in our time, and it has had its impact in precisely the terms which Alan Lomax described in the preface: "This treasury is the first attempt to set up a canon for American folksong, defining the world of people's music in terms of examples and placing the songs in their historical, social, and psychological backgrounds." The collection is clearly the final fruit of the Lomaxes' attempt to delineate the nature and significance of a distinctly American body of song, but it also provides us with an opportunity to note the changes in approach since the days of *Cowboy Songs.*

The most important change is the slighting of the ballad as an exclusive category of folksong. Although ballads are included in *Folk Song: U.S.A.* and the editors describe singers as "ballad-makers," they point out that "Such British ballads as 'Barbara Allen' were not included since our object was to show what American singers had created, not what they had preserved." The distinction is important: it does not deny that British balladry existed in America. But it is a point of view that clearly marks the break with the hegemony of the British ballad. In place of the idea that the ballad is the beginning and end of American folksong research, the editors substituted the notion of a variety of "themes, tunes, types and styles of folk music" which characterize the American tradition. At the same time, the Lomaxes argue strongly that folksong is an art in itself, rather than simply the source of formal literature. The affirmation comes almost parenthetically: "Folk song, as art of all serious intent, improves on acquaintance." A lifetime of collecting by John Lomax had provided the materials which made it possible for his son to write: "These songs that lived to walk the long, lonesome road with the people have been largely written down by folklorists during the past fifty years. The 'best' of these, the most 'representative'—our favorites after years of collecting and singing—we have chosen for *Folk Song: U.S.A.* For beauty, variety, strength, and singability, these 111 songs will, we believe, stand alongside any songs from any nation or level of culture." That it was still necessary to affirm the value of American folksong in comparison with the folk art of other nations is testimony to the fact that the Lomaxes were faced with essentially the same problem that confronted Emerson and Whitman; even this late in our history, it was necessary to identify the nature of an American art and the sources from which it sprang.

At the center of John and Alan Lomax's conception of the uniqueness of American folksong is a democratic affirmation which also underscores their affinity with the Emerson-Whitman tradition. The statement by the Lomaxes of the importance of democratic processes in the development of American folksong proceeded along the following lines. In place of the oversimplified and outmoded conception of the communal origin of folksongs (an idea devastated by innumerable critics), the Lomaxes presented the idea of continual change, whereby, over a long period of time, the song is emended by countless singers and finally becomes a true folk product: "So the *mass* of a people participate in a folk song's growth, forever reweaving old materials to create new versions, much as an old lady creates a new quilt out of an old by adding, year by year, new scraps and patches. So folk song grows in small steps, with every slight change tested for audience reaction, thereby achieving a permanence in man's affection matched only by the greatest art. This art lives upon the lips of the multitude and is transmitted by the grapevine, surviving sometimes for centuries because it reflects so well the deepest emotional convictions of the common man. This is truly democratic art, painting a portrait of the people, unmatched for honesty and validity in any other record." This description of how folksong becomes communal is not especially new; but the value judgment placed on the process marks a revival of Herder's original view of the vitality and significance of folksong. At the same time the statement echoes Whitman's concern with the "en masse" and the creation of democratic audiences. One need only bear in mind the generations of folklorists who, operating on the basis of a romanticized version of Herder's ideas, lost all sight of his conception of the close relationship between folksong and democracy. Then the significance of the Lomaxes' formulations take on their full meaning and we discover yet another instance of the Americans' continued insight into the deepest levels of Herder's thought. And just as Whitman was convinced that the unique contribution of America to the history of the world was to be its raising of common humanity to the highest level of importance, so the leading motif in American folksong, according to the Lomaxes, is the glorification of the common man: "The common man has always held the center of the stage in our balladry. From Paul Bunyan to Jesse James, the folklore heroes are brave, free-hearted, and handy on the job. A good hand was welcome and respected at the campfire, no matter what his race or religion, while a gent with 'high-toned' airs was headed for certain trouble. Long before Whitman, American folksingers rhapsodized the common man in all his dazzling variety, putting him first in all the ballads, describing him at work and play, and making his passions and problems their main concern." The reference to Whitman is not accidental, nor is his significance so casual as Lomax makes it seem. To be sure Whitman is not unique in his avowal of American democracy. Yet it was Whitman who developed most fully the notion that a native culture must rest on the creative power of the common man. Similarly Lomax identified the major theme of American folksong in equalitarian terms: "This is the big theme of American folk song, running through all the songs—the theme stated by Burns's '. . . A man's a man for a' that' and even more powerfully in the Negro ballad, 'John Henry.' *A man ain't nothin' but a man. . . .*"[17]

In his own commitment to this theme the folklorist "goes where book-learning is not. He lives with the underprivileged. He brings back the proof in their songs and stories and dances that these folks are expressive and concerned about the beautiful and the good. In doing so, he continually denies the validity of caste lines and class barriers. Malinowski says of the anthropologist, 'He also has the duty to speak as the native's advocate.' Just so, the folklorist has the duty to speak as the advocate of the common man." What Malinowski had in mind was clearly something like the equality of cultures, however incommensurate, and we can recognize this as an impact from Herder's earlier formulation. But we need also to recognize in Lomax's position a close approximation of Emerson's definition of the American scholar. The folklorist is not an impartial observer or a collector of ancient manuscripts; for him too life is a dictionary and, as we shall see, his involvement in the actual conditions of folk life brings him inevitably into conflict with the more refined atmosphere of academic research. Ultimately the folklorist becomes a man whose mission is to announce the importance of the common man to the nations of the world. It was precisely in this respect that Negro folksong took on symbolic meaning for the Lomaxes. The Negro's music was not outside American folksong, as earlier collectors had concluded. The numerous field recordings collected by John and Alan Lomax showed clearly the rhythmic and melodic impact of black folk music on *every area* of American folksong, from the folk hymn to the blues. Even more important was the fact that black folk music represented the highest statement of the theme of freedom, which for the Lomaxes (as for Emerson and Whitman) is the leading motif in American thought. Thus, although Alan Lomax recognized the profound prejudice against the Negro in America, the merging of white and black folk traditions revealed a unity that undercut surface tensions: "The tremendous popularity of 'John Henry,' 'Frankie,' and other Negro ballads among white singers, the tremendous enthusiasm of all Americans, no matter what their prejudices, for Negro folk music, and the profound influences of this music on American culture—all this denies the effect of Jim Crow at this level of human communication. From the beginning, Negroes and whites have swapped tunes, tales, dances, and religious ideas. And in the even more basic areas of speech and motor behavior this meeting of minds between two groups is clearer still. White Americans, perhaps at first attracted by the exotic rhythms and earthy poesy of Negro song, have been deeply stirred by the poignant sorrow, the biting irony. and the noble yearning for a better world implicit there." Negro folksong best illustrated the hybridization which characterized American folk tradition, and it is worth recalling how close this formulation is to the views of Constance Rourke, or the comment by Whitman about the "polyglot" nature of our literary expression. Indeed, for the Lomaxes it was the merging of West African and British folk styles that accounted for the unique qualities of American folksong; it was a cultural integration that lay beneath even the most obvious political disparities between white and black. In form as well as in content, Negro folk music epitomized the achievement of American folk art, and because of the components from black tradition there was an emphasis as well on the American impulse toward equality. The Lomaxes are even closer to Emerson and Whitman in their awareness that this was a reflection of the struggle of all Americans to realize the promise of our democratic traditions. (This is precisely the view of Ralph Ellison's black narrator, who concludes *Invisible Man* with the comment, "Who knows but that, on the lower frequencies, I speak for you?")

Finally, as Herder himself had demonstrated when he published his collection of international folksongs, the democratic force of folk culture leads to an affirmation of internationalism. When the American folksinger is understood, according to Lomax, "when you come to know him, you will be prepared to meet his kinfolk in Russia, China, Spain, Ireland, or wherever oral song lives, for in song and folklore one encounters ancient bonds that link the races and the nations into the big family of humanity." With this statement we have, in a sense, come full circle—from Herder's conception of *Humanität* to Lomax's view of the family of humanity. In their attitudes toward nationalism, the democratic affirmation of folksong, the persistence of folk art within sophisticated societies, the organic relationship of folklore to the land, and the elevation of national culture to the level of internationalism—in all these John and Alan Lomax can be seen to be the intellectual heirs of Herder. The influence of course is not direct; yet the number of similarities is too great to be overlooked.

But if it illustrates, as I have suggested, the continuity of European ideas in American thought, it emphasizes as well their remolding to fit the needs of the American experience. It is essential to recall, therefore, that the Lomaxes also represent the American scholar in our own time; despite the century which separates them, the Lomaxes faced intellectual problems identical with those that confronted Emerson and Whitman. That they evolved answers of a similar nature is not simply adventitious. It is testimony to the historical continuity of thought in regard to the function and significance of folk art in a democratic society. In their defiance of the Child ballad tradition, their insistence on the integrity of American materials, and in their marked democratic ideology, the Lomaxes can be placed clearly in the framework of the Emerson-Whitman tradition.

The inability of critics to evaluate the Lomaxes' work comes in part from the tendency in American thought to fragment our experience and underestimate the continuity of our history. American life has changed so fast and so often that historical relationships, so easily discernible in other more stable cultures, are obscured in our own. At the same time, the Lomaxes have raised problems for folklorists similar to those faced by literary critics of Emerson and, especially, Whitman. An early critic put it most clearly when, commenting on John Lomax's strategy of collecting songs in the prisons of the South, he complained: ". . . as a result of this novel procedure, the book of Messrs. Lomax gives one at first the impression that America depends for its folksong literature chiefly on 'Niggah' convicts and white 'bums.' "[18] It may indeed be embarrassing for America that its most active folklorists identified our folksongs with the lowest orders of society. Far from being idiosyncratic, however, the attitudes of the Lomaxes toward the relationship between folksong and democracy need to be seen as part of the continuing effort by Americans to identify the nature of a national, democratic culture. What many of their critics have failed to see is their frankly ideological position that the creation of folk art by the common man *ought* to be used as a justification of political democracy. Their assumptions should be subjected to scrutiny. But unless, as one writer has suggested, we have truly come to an end of ideology, the Lomaxes' endeavors must first be seen as a conscious and significant effort to discover the roots and to define the meaning of American folk culture and its implications for our society as a whole.

In the period following the end of the Second World War a good many developments took place which substantiated the views of Constance Rourke and the Lomaxes. In *The Folk Songs of North America*

(1960), Lomax maps the range of American folksongs on a regional basis, noting the "democratic pressure" which broke down inherited styles and worked hand in hand with the musical nonconformity of American folksingers and musicians. He also takes into account the difference between the restrictive tendencies of white Protestantism and the freer sexual attitudes revealed in Negro secular music. "The founders and the carriers of American hot music were, of course, the Negroes," he points out. "Their West African culture encouraged songs and dances which gave a pleasurable community outlet to sexual and aggressive behaviour. Such release of tension probably accounts for the exquisite rhythmic ability and the vocal relaxation and freedom of good Negro singers, as compared with those of other cultures. . . . This is no primitive trait. Both the Negro and his songs are complex and civilized. The folk Negro in Africa and America, as a child and as an adult, can *play* at being hostile or sexy in singing and in conversation, and no one thinks the worse of him. So he can play with a melody, shaping it to his changing moods, gracing it with all the colour of a relaxed voice." Lomax found himself impressed by the paganism and eroticism which persisted in British folk tradition to the present day, but which had been struck out in this country by the "pioneer folk censor." Yet the "full weight of Puritanism did not fall upon the Negroes, who came from cultures which placed a high value on erotic and aggressive behaviour and which provided outlets for them in song, dance, and ceremonial. As slaves and later, as second-class citizens in the South, they were not expected to conform rigidly to the conventions that harassed the whites. Even the country Baptist preachers looked on sex as one thing and sin as another. At the folk level, especially, the Negro escaped some of the anxieties and conflicts that plagued white Americans, and his often joyous, always sensuous music shows it." What the Lomaxes had defined earlier as the essential theme of Negro folksong—the longing for freedom—had pushed them into a narrower statement than the materials of Negro music suggested. The idea of freedom in his religious music subsumed another marked affirmation in Negro secular songs, especially blues. Alan Lomax early acknowledged the major impact of blues on all areas of American folk and popular music as well as jazz. (His classic study, *Mister Jelly Roll* [1950] traced the lines of contact between black folk culture and New Orleans jazz.) But only later did he extend the conception to a full balance of the meanings implicit in the religious and secular traditions. A critic of the Lomaxes' ideological position could, with some justice, point out that the major motifs in the blues are obviously concerned with love, death, and eroticism

—conceptions which do not seem to fit into the broad political patterns of the spirituals. Lomax later provided a more subtle analysis of both elements. "Few folk songs," he points out in *The Folk Songs of North America,* are directly political: "Some songs hint at a deep ground swell of response to major social changes. . . . But normally folk songs change slowly and mysteriously, rooted as they are in fundamental social and psychological patterns that resist alteration. New versions and variants arise ceaselessly as the songs are passed on by word of mouth, and the study of these versions has fascinated scholars. To my way of thinking, however, we do not yet understand enough about the unconscious processes at work in the slow emergence of versions to control such studies."

Yet Lomax continued to define the main thrust of American folksong in terms of the hybridization of British and West African folk traditions. At the same time, his revaluation of the meaning of Negro folksong brought him into even closer accord with the ideological position of Whitman, who, as we have seen, attempted to define the meaning of American culture in terms of political freedom and a program for sexual candor. Both those ideas have continued to make themselves felt in recent revivals of interest in folksong and the popular song traditions derived from them. Indeed that continuing infusion of characteristically black styles into the mainstream of American music has been noticeable in the past twenty years, a period during which authentic styles of white and Negro tradition received close attention as well. This most recent folk boom has substantiated most of the views of Constance Rourke and the Lomaxes. I date it from about 1949, the time when several folk-based songs became nationally, and then internationally, known through the recordings of commercially oriented as well as traditional singers. Such groups as the Weavers and the Kingston Trio fulfilled the function of earlier interpreters of folksong and especially Negro songs, gaining for the first time in history not merely regional audiences but national and international ones as well. Traditional singers such as Huddie Ledbetter, Woody Guthrie, and others found themselves capable of attracting remarkably large audiences. Characteristically, the popular life-span of the traditional singers (and especially the Negro singers) was relatively short, while the commercially oriented groups (most of them white) were able to last much longer. One major result of this recent folk revival was perceptively analyzed by Alan Lomax: "No wonder then that a part of the captive audience of the entertainment industry is turning to folk song. These young skifflers and banjo pickers are sick of listening passively. They want to make music of their own. Some know that it is dangerous for them to express their discontent in a political direction, and so, for the moment, the tuneful complaints of their forebears voice their rebellious feelings. Having identified themselves with the democratic musical traditions of their country, they go on to make their own topical songs, and some of these modern ballads may have the staying power of the old." But even more important, Lomax continues, "a whole generation of creative young people are becoming expert practitioners of our native folk song and thus are coming to grips with the profoundest American emotional problems." We can see even better today that one of the major results of the folksong revival was the renaissance of interest in the authentic styles of American folk instruments, including the five-string banjo, guitar, Appalachian dulcimer, and blues harmonica. And although enthusiasm for the traditional styles fluctuates, it never quite disappears, as the work of every new generation of singers and song composers reveals.

At the same time, music continued to play a major ideological role in the civil rights movements of the fifties and sixties, illustrating the staying power of black folk tradition for the nation at large. The younger generation of blacks in the South had apparently lost contact with the religious music of their ancestors. One was tempted to agree with the oft-repeated assertions that traditional black music was fast disappearing and would soon exist only as museum relics. But even the most casual observer of events connected with the movement for equal rights in the South (and elsewhere) could see that the legacy of black song functioned as the central statement of the movement's significance. "We Shall Overcome," a church song mainly sung in the deep South, became the national anthem for blacks and whites who were committed to bringing into reality the existence of full citizenship for all Americans. Many were startled when the President of the United States, a white Southerner, chose to incorporate the title of the song in a major speech defining the national stance with regard to civil rights.[18] (Others, it might be added, were incensed at what they considered his attempt to "co-opt" it.)

That cultural integration of blacks and whites which the Lomaxes identified has continued to manifest itself to an extraordinary degree in the last several decades, despite the development of other strategies such as black nationalism and the continuing separatist positions of many whites. The persistent infusion of black styles into our music will hardly accomplish by itself the full implementation of equalitarian principles, but it continues to illustrate a major tendency to identify the folklore of a supposed outcast and lowly segment of our people as the locus of the highest spiritual and esthetic values. That movement, first affirmed by Emerson and Whitman, was reinforced and expanded by the work of John and Alan Lomax.[19]

Chapter Six
The Blues as a Literary Theme

THE USE of folklore by American writers is a subject that has been discussed only briefly. Daniel Hoffman's *Form and Fable in American Fiction* (1961) is the most successful attempt to understand the impact on our early writers of themes and techniques related to folk tradition, and he has gone far toward correcting the view that folklore has counted for little in our literary developments. My concern here will be with the use of Negro folklore and folksong in more recent works which reflect both the ideological and technical implications of folklore as a basis for literary expression. One area of special interest is jazz and themes related to its origin and development.

It has been widely noted that there is a special relationship between the Negro and the American experience in general. For one thing, it is important to recall that of all the diverse groups who came to this country only the blacks came in large numbers against their will and under conditions of chattel slavery. David Brion Davis has pointed out that while slavery posed a general moral problem for all of Western culture, it had special relevance in the New World. His major conclusion in *The Problem of Slavery in Western Culture* (1966) is that the central patterns of slavery in all cultures have been more like than unlike, yet there is a sense in which slavery came close to defining the very meaning of the "American mission." He observes that "Americans have often been embarrassed when reminded that the Declaration of Independence was written by a slaveholder and that Negro slavery was a legal institution in all thirteen colonies at the beginning of the revolution." Critics of America's national aspirations have made the most of what is an obvious contradiction and inconsistency in our equalitarian ideology, and Davis shows in his study how widely spread were the rationalizations used to justify the existence of slavery within the context of a democratic society such as the United States claimed to be. His explorations stop short of the abolitionist period in this country, concluding with the prophecy of Quaker John Woolman that "if Americans continued to be unfaithful to their high destiny, their descendants would face the awful retribution of God's justice." In general, and to the present day, Americans have relied on standard rationalizations to justify either slavery or the separation of blacks from the mainstream of American life. Several of our major folklorists (Constance Rourke and the Lomaxes), on the other hand, have attempted to find a central position for the Negro and his accomplishments within the framework of American civilization, emphasizing the seminal influence of Negro folk materials. Most academic folklorists, however, tended to place black tradition outside the main lines of American development, identifying it either as African or as mere imitation of white traditions.

Our formal writers have often taken a rather different approach. Mark Twain, for example, used Jim in *Huckleberry Finn* as a way of expressing strong opposition to the hypocrisy of middle-class American society. Hoffman has pointed out that Jim rises above the stereotyped notion of the fearful slave to become "a source of moral energy," though he also recognizes that "Mark Twain's triumph here is incomplete: despite the skillful gradation of folk beliefs and other indications of Jim's emergent stature, what does come through for many readers is, as Mr. Ellison remarks, Jim's boy-to-boy relationship with Huck, 'a violation of our conception of adult maleness.' We remember that Mark Twain himself admired Uncle Remus extravagantly, and much as he means for us to admire Jim—much as he admires Jim himself—the portrait, though drawn in deepest sympathy, is yet seen from the outside." I shall return later to Ralph Ellison's comments about Negro folklore and American literature. But it is interesting to see what that outsider's view of the Negro has meant not only for the characterization of blacks in our literature, but also for the uses of Negro folklore as well. Curiously, one of the main purposes of employing Negro materials by many of our writers has been ideological—as a way of establishing some sense of the world view of non-Negro characters in fiction.

Some obvious examples from the period after the First World War come to mind, and they illustrate the general approach. Most of them take place in the context of the "jazz age," and they provide a good contrast between white writers who know little about the history or meaning of jazz and those later writers whose knowledge of jazz and its folk sources are more sophisticated. F. Scott Fitzgerald limns a scene early in *The Great Gatsby* (1925) which is calculated to dramatize the opulence and emptiness of American society in the twenties. At one of Gatsby's wild parties the orchestra leader announces: " 'At the request of Mr. Gatsby we are going to play for you Mr. Vladimir Tostoff's latest work which attracted so much attention at Carnegie Hall last May. If you read the papers, you know there was a big sensation.' He smiled with jovial condescension, and added: 'Some sensation!' Whereupon everybody laughed. 'The piece is known,'

he concluded lustily, 'as Vladimir Tostoff's *Jazz History of the World.*' "
Fitzgerald's narrator comments that when it was over "girls were putting their heads on men's shoulders in a puppyish, convivial way,
girls were swooning over backward playfully into men's arms, even
into groups, knowing that some one would arrest their falls . . . ,"
though Gatsby himself remains aloof from the activities. Despite the
fact that we get no description of the work, it is easy to piece together the nuances of the passage. The performance of the work was
a sensation—apparently a scandalous occasion in the major hall associated with symphonic music and recitals. The composer's name
suggests why: it is a piece simply tossed off, which is a close approximation of the main criticism of jazz, namely that it is not carefully or consciously composed but simply a kind of musical fling.
(The less pejorative term would be *improvised,* which is an accurate
way of defining one of the essential elements in jazz performances.)
A Jazz History of the World would have been an assault on the very
idea of history itself, expressing the lack of order with an equally
shocking disregard of conventional musical sound—cacophonous,
perhaps polyrhythmic, and above all sensual in its appeal, as the
orchestra leader's "lusty" introduction and the following aphrodisi-
acal effects reveal. (Fitzgerald may have been referring to one of
Igor Stravinsky's early works which were received with great hostility in the first part of this century precisely because they contained
innumerable innovations, including techniques borrowed from jazz.)
The important point is that jazz is defined in essentially negative terms
as a way of identifying the chaos and libertinism of Gatsby's world,
and although the composer is obviously a Russian, the controlling elements of his work depend on their relationship to jazz, a Negro music.

Fitzgerald's interest in what he calls jazz as well as in popular music
reminds us how rarely American writers use music thematically in
their work, unlike European writers (Mann, for example) who often
derive major elements of their form and content through conscious
analogies with music. (Whitman, as has been widely noted, is an exception, and so is Eliot.) There are, however, a great number of references to popular songs in *The Great Gatsby* and they generally
reflect the uncommitted, lackadaisical attitudes of Fitzgerald's characters—other than Gatsby, of course, who pays little attention to the
surface atmosphere which he has caused to be created. The tunes
include "The Sheik of Araby," "Ain't We Got Fun," "Three O'Clock
in the Morning," and "The Love Nest," several of these performed
by Gatsby's boarder, Mr. Klipspringer. In a flashback which details
Gatsby's early involvement with Daisy in Louisville, Fitzgerald wrote:

"For Daisy was young and her artificial world was redolent of orchids and pleasant, cheerful snobbery and orchestras which set the rhythm of the year, summing up the madness and suggestiveness of life in new tunes. All night long the saxophones wailed the hopeless comment of the *Beale Street Blues* while a hundred pairs of golden slippers shuffled the shining dust." Shortly thereafter Fitzgerald announces Daisy's decision to marry Tom Buchanan. Again it is apparent that the music reflects the hollowness of Daisy's environment and although Fitzgerald identifies the pop tunes with sadness as well as the possibilities of new life, the clinching reference is to the "hopeless comment" of the blues. All of these statements amount to an ideological position which appears regularly in American literature thereafter, probably through the influence of Fitzgerald, though he was familiar with Eliot's similar approach in *The Waste Land* (1922): "When lovely woman stoops to folly and/ Paces about her room again, alone,/ She smoothes her hair with automatic hand,/ And puts a record on the gramaphone." On the one hand, we might define this position as the use of popular songs to provide incidental music for the decline of man's vitality and sensibility in the modern world. The pop tune works marvelously in this manner, for it is technically slight (a simple formula defines almost all the compositions) and its diction illustrates perfectly a cloying, sentimental tone that contrasts obviously with the achievements of "serious" poetry.

But even as we identify these elements of commercial, popular music, it is apparent that it contributes something else to the values asserted by writers such as Fitzgerald—and we might add Hemingway, Dos Passos, and Faulkner, among others. However trite and barbaric the music appears to be, it functions nevertheless as a lever against the cultural pretensions of conventional middle-class society. And it does so, I would suggest, not so much for its own sake as for its association with a tradition of which it is a heavily watered down version—namely, Negro jazz and its folk sources. Despite their limited awareness of the nature and sources of American music, some sense of what underlay the popular songs leaked through in the work of writers like Fitzgerald. Jazz carried clear associations with a level of culture decidedly outside the stream of middle-class white morality and rooted essentially in the attitudes and expression of the Negro. For the writers of the twenties and thirties jazz carried strong connotations and was associated with stereotypes of the Negro as fantastically virile and barbarously effective in his sexual life. Attempts to pinpoint the etymology of the word have failed to produce a clear explanation, but all discover a primary use of jazz (sometimes *jass*) as a verb meaning to fornicate.

The Jazz Age (the coinage seems in fact to have been Fitzgerald's) picked up all these nuances: the disillusionment with the Great War, the reaction to Prohibition and associated "puritanical" restrictions of the period, the wide open life of the speakeasies with their flow of bootleg liquor and promiscuous women—though the latter are always underplayed in our nostalgic recreations of the period, in films particularly. Although Negroes appear occasionally (as musicians) the Jazz Age is presented to us in literature from the disaffected white's point of view; what it suggests to us about the Negro himself is a form of sentimental primitivism: jazz is his music and the white listener uses it as a way of making some small contact with the jungle madness which its beat suggests. The sense of distance is important, for while jazz is conceived to be a threat to the values of the sick world in the period after the First World War, it is also the fitting accompaniment for its impending demise. Tostoff's composition is ironically only the other side of Tom Buchanan's assertion: " 'Civilization's going to pieces. . . . I've gotten to be a terrible pessimist about things. Have you read "The Rise of the Colored Empires" by this man Goddard? . . . Well it's a fine book, and everybody ought to read it. The idea is if we don't look out the white race will be—will be utterly submerged. It's all scientific stuff; it's been proved.' " *The Jazz History of the World* is the finale for the last act.

William Faulkner's response to music is in general very much like Fitzgerald's. But occasionally he gives us a view of Negro music (and folklore) which is much less patronizing than that of his contemporaries, and at times he comes close to folkloristic precision. Ralph Ellison has noted in *Shadow and Act* (1964) that, despite his ambivalence and his willingness to accept major stereotypes of the Negro, Faulkner "has explored perhaps more successfully than anyone else, either white or black, certain forms of Negro humanity." In part this is due to his remarkably prolific exploration of the South in general, but Ellison observes that Faulkner's central quest is for human truth rather than regional or racial insights. Because the social order of the South "harms whites no less than blacks, the sensitive Southerner, the artist, is apt to feel its effects acutely—and within the deepest levels of his personality. For not only is the social division forced upon the Negro by the ritualized ethic of discrimination, but upon the white man by the strictly enforced set of anti-Negro taboos. The conflict is always within him. Indeed, so rigidly has the recognition of Negro humanity been tabooed that the white Southerner is apt to associate any form of personal rebellion with the Negro. So that for the Southern artist the Negro becomes a symbol of his personal rebellion, his guilt and his repression of it. The Negro is thus a compelling object of fascination, and this we see very clearly in Faulkner." Since Faulkner has also recognized how inextricably the Negro is involved in the meaning of America itself, he has often taken an approach somewhat different from Fitzgerald's. At the same time, like many of our Southern writers, he is closer to the roots of Negro folk tradition and often reproduces elements from it with great accuracy, as we can see from some descriptions of black music in his novels. *Sartoris* (1929) was Faulkner's third novel but the first in which he found his distinctive voice and most of his major themes. It abounds in Negro stereotypes—"his race's fine feeling for potential theatrics," "the grave and simple pleasure of his race." But it also contains some prime examples of the quality, style, and range of black music. Elnora, the house servant, sings snatches of spirituals "as she soused her mop into the pail and thumped it on the floor again."

> Sinner riz fum de moaner's bench,
> Sinner jump to de penance bench;
> When de preacher ax 'im whut de reason why,
> Say, "Preacher got de women jes' de same ez I."
>   Oh, Lawd, oh, Lawd!
> Dat's whut de matter wid de church today.

On other occasions Elnora's voice floats "in meaningless minor suspense" or wells "in mellow falling suspense"—a description which catches nicely the melismatic quality of Negro singing as it moves from tone to tone, rarely stopping squarely on a given pitch.

In another section young Bayard puts together a Negro trio to provide an evening serenade: "They stopped here, in shadow. The Negroes descended and lifted the bass viol out, and a guitar. The third one held a slender tube frosted over the keys upon which the intermittent moon glinted in pale points, and they stood with their heads together, murmuring among themselves and touching plaintive muted chords from the strings. . . . The tunes were old tunes. Some of them were sophisticated tunes and formally intricate, but in the rendition this was lost and all of them were imbued instead with a plaintive similarity, a slurred and rhythmic simplicity; fading, dying in minor reiterations along the treacherous vistas of the moon." The performance ends with "Home, Sweet Home" and a rendition of "Good Night, Ladies," sung in the "true, oversweet tenor" of one of the white men who accompany the Negroes. (Faulkner refers to the rich *minor* of "Home, Sweet Home" although it is actually in a major key. Yet the rendition of this standard sentimental tune by a black group could easily give it a minor tonality.) But as in much of his work, Faulkner is perhaps more accurate than he knew, because the description of Negroes appropriating materials from the general culture into their own style is a precise illustration of that hybridization of diverse materials which defines the quality of American folksong. (It recalls Alan Lomax's observation that the major elements in American folksong derive from West African and British sources combined uniquely in the United States.)

Finally there is Bayard's response to the movements of country Negroes through the town at noon: "—Negroes slow and aimless as figures of a dark placid dream, with an animal odor, murmuring and laughing among themselves; there was in their consonantless murmuring something ready with mirth, in their laughter something grave and sad. . . ." Bayard continues to watch: "Against the wall, squatting, a blind Negro beggar, with a guitar and a wire frame holding a mouth-organ to his lips, patterned the background of smells and sounds with a plaintive reiteration of rich, monotonous chords, rhythmic as a mathematical formula, but without music. He was a man of at least forty and his was that patient resignation of many sightless years. . . ." Bayard groped for a coin in his pocket "and the beggar sensed his approach and his tune became a single repeated chord, but without a break in the rhythm, until the coin rang into the cup, and still without a break in the rhythm and the meaningless strains of the mouth-organ, his left hand dropped groping a little to the cup and read the coin in a single motion; then once more guitar and mouth-organ resumed their monotonous pattern." What Faulkner had caught here is the central tradition of Negro folksong—the blues. In fact, one of the main sources of its dispersion through the South was the blind street singer such as the one described in the passage, and Faulkner is exceptionally accurate in his description of what the music sounded like; it is indeed a heavily rhythmic, formulaic repetition of standard motifs, though more complex than Faulkner suggests. The combination of guitar and mouth-organ is a traditional one—in the South the harmonica is more likely to be called a French harp, I think because it is tongued and hence by analogy from French kiss. In any case, the style associated with blues harmonica is a major innovation of Southern blacks. It is accomplished by playing the instrument in a key different from the one in which it is tuned, which results in a striking blues tonality ordinarily not possible on the instrument, which is nonchromatic and has a very limited range. As in some of his other comments about black music and singing Faulkner refers to meaningless strains, and of course, having omitted any reference to the singing which would accompany the blues, he misses the verbal comment as well as the complex relationship between instrumental and vocal styles that is inherent in the country blues. In other words, Faulkner is still far from understanding fully the meaning or the function of blues in black tradition, and he uses the music to underscore the disaffection of his lost-generation protagonist, Bayard Sartoris. Yet he comes closer to the materials than any writer up to his time, just as in *The Sound and the Fury* (1929) he gives us one of the best descriptions of a Negro singing sermon which has ever been presented in American literature. The Reverend Shegog begins in the standard speech of educated Southerners and then suddenly breaks into a country dialect: " 'Breddren en sistuhn!' His voice rang again, with the horns. He removed his arm and stood erect and raised his hands. 'I got de ricklickshun en de blood of de lamb!' They did not mark just when his intonation, his pronunciation became negroid, they just sat swaying a little in their seats as the voice took them into itself." It is a perceptive insight into the pluralistic pattern of American Negro life, and when the disguise is lifted Shegog fits immediately into the pattern of call and response which is basic to Negro folksong and folk sermons, the preacher half-speaking and half-singing, in response to the occasional cries and melodic intonations of the congregation.

But while Faulkner's is a significant accomplishment, it yet falls short of fulfilling the possibilities of Negro materials for their own sake as well as for what they can tell us of American life in general. We can see this best by looking closely at Ralph Ellison's *Invisible Man* (1952), which defines the ideological and technical possibilities of American Negro materials more accurately and effectively than any work in our literary history. Ellison is valuable also because he is one of those writers whose criticism is as carefully crafted as his fiction—it is a virtue we often associate with poets (from Dryden to Eliot) but which, with the major exception of Henry James, seems less prevalent among fiction writers.

To begin with, it is important to recognize that Ellison does not conceive the book as a "Negro novel" in any sense of the term. What he has learned from Faulkner is that the relationships between black and white are central to the meaning of *American* development. That does not prevent him from understanding the unique qualities of Negro life and culture, but it does mark him from the tendency discernible in some Negro writers to associate themselves with separatism or Black Nationalism. Ellison explains his position partly from the fact that his roots are in the Southwest rather than in the deep South, though it seems to me he could have arrived at a similar conclusion even if he had been brought up in the Black Belt. Still it is important for him to recall (in *Shadow and Act*) that as a boy he and his companions felt little of the pressure to move inwardly toward the ghetto and away from the possibilities of American life: "Contrary to the notion currently projected by certain specialists in the 'Negro problem' which characterizes the Negro American as self-hating and defensive, we did not so regard ourselves. We felt, among ourselves at least, that we were supposed to be whoever we would and could be and do anything and everything which other boys did, and do it better. Not defensively, because we were ordered to do so; not because it was held in the society at large that we were naturally, as Negroes, limited—but because we demanded it of ourselves. Because to measure up to our own standards was the only way of affirming our notion of manhood." This is in line with Ellison's general conception of the meaning of American life which, as I think can be made clearer from the novel, is closest to the ideas of Emerson. Consequently, he points out, it was perfectly logical for him and his companions to think of themselves as Renaissance men, just as white Southerners viewed themselves as ancient Greeks or Cavaliers: "Surely our fantasies have caused far less damage to the nation's sense of reality, if for no other reason than that ours were expressions of a more democratic ideal. Remember, too, as William Faulkner made us so vividly aware, that the slaves often took the essence of the aristocratic ideal (as they took Christianity) with far more seriousness than their masters, and that we, thanks to the tight telescoping of American history, were but two generations from that previous condition." Ellison's point is that the Negro has never really been out of the mainstream of American experience, despite continuing assertions that the Negro is best understood as a man without a past: his African inheritance stripped away, this argument insists, there was nothing capable of replacing it in a society which consciously kept him hermetically sealed in the ghetto. Ellison's formulation is familiar—indeed it is another version of the frontier hypothesis: "One thing is certain, ours was a chaotic community, still characterized by frontier attitudes and by that strange mixture of the naive and sophisticated, the benign and malignant, which makes the American past so puzzling and its present so confusing; that mixture which often affords the minds of the young who grow up in the far provinces such wide and unstructured latitude, and which encourages the individual's imagination—up to the moment 'reality' closes in upon him—to range widely and, sometimes, even to soar." Like pioneer Americans, the Negro lost elements of his inherited background but assimilated others from the materials available to him in this country.

Ellison uses just these circumstances to point out how closely the Negro's experience reproduces that of the American's. In response to a critic's attempt to define the Negro as a primitive "trickster," Ellison argues that the Negro uses the mask precisely as all Americans have, in the context of "the old American problem of identity." For the American, as Constance Rourke pointed out, was always defined as a "barbarian" who had left his claim to culture in the Old World. The idea of the smart man playing dumb is a strategy hardly limited to Negroes. "Actually," Ellison notes, "it is a role which Negroes share with other Americans, and it might be more 'Yankee' than anything else. It is a strategy common to the culture. . . . The white American has charged the Negro American with being without a past or tradition (something which strikes him with nameless horror), just as he himself has been so charged by European and American critics with a nostalgia for the stability of European cultures; and the Negro knows that both were 'mammy-made' right here at home. What's more, each secretly believes that he alone knows what is valid in the American experience, and the other knows he knows, but will not admit it, and each suspects the other of being at bottom a phony."[2] This is a version of what I called "The Arkansas Traveler" strategy of humor, in which the American faces his critic by pretending to be even dumber than he is expected to be, all the while undercutting his opponent by a play of witty *double-entendre*.

But Ellison goes even farther along folkloristic lines. As he has suggested, one of his essential interests is in the revelation of the peculiarly American problem of identity. Many of our writers and critics have turned to folklore as a way of answering some of the questions that problem raises; and Ellison takes the same tack, though here we are in a position to see how the strategy will work in the context of black folk tradition. The general approach, however, is the same one that I have traced to Herder. It uses folk tradition as the basis for an understanding of the national character, and in this case it becomes possible to examine closely the roots of Negro folklore in order to discern the elements that have formed major segments of American Negro expression. (At the same time, Ellison understands the Negro to represent some essential qualities of the American himself—as Constance Rourke and the Lomaxes had already argued in their own versions of Herderian folk ideology.) Yet another major connection is apparent when Ellison notes that his major interest is literary and he explains that his concern with folklore is primarily for what it will allow him to do as a writer: "I use folklore in my work not because I am Negro, but because writers like Eliot and Joyce made me conscious of the literary value of my folk inheritance. My cultural background, like that of most Americans, is dual (my middle name, sadly enough, is Waldo). . . . My point is that the Negro American writer is also an heir of the human experience which is literature, and this might well be more important to him than his living folk tradition. For me, at least, in the discontinuous, swiftly changing and diverse American culture, the stability of the Negro American folk tradition became precious as a result of an act of literary discovery." Ralph Waldo Ellison is a lot closer politically and esthetically to his namesake than he has admitted. More importantly, and despite his valid objection to being construed as a folk writer, he has given us a major illustration of how the American writer uses folk materials to create a distinctly national expression which yet speaks in broadly human rather than racial or regional terms. These are the values I have examined in previous sections of this study. Ellison not only brings us up to date; he is an effective and impressive heir to what has gone before, filling in outlines of crucial areas that had only been sketched earlier.

Ellison's central concern in *Invisible Man* is to provide a portrait of the American and his focusing on a black hero raises at once that peculiarly American formulation which we have encountered earlier. The American is conceived to be a man without a past or anterior folk-lore which will serve to define his national values and literary expression. If this is true for the American in general, it is especially true for the Negro—and Ellison's point is that his situation is the same as his white counterpart's. But the circumstances of his attempt to define his identity will be framed by his relationships to the white world, which functions in relation to the Negro as the European world operated in regard to the white American. The hero, in short, is *peau rouge* whatever the actual color of his skin. And he is also the American barbarian, although the source of barbarism in this case is not the frontier but the jungle heritage of Africa. In the face of this collection of stereotypes, the hero assumes the mask as a means of undercutting the assumptions of his adversaries. The next step is predictable: as the American in general needs to show that his tradition is rich and meaningful, so the American Negro needs to convince himself and his critics that black folk tradition is more than the mumbo-jumbo or the cacophony that jazz is usually taken to be. The dynamic of the novel stems from the hero's struggle with himself to acknowledge the legitimacy of his heritage in the face of constant attacks by the white community or its allies in the society of Negroes. Nothing is simple and the virtue of Ellison's comic strategy is that it cuts both ways, undermining the stereotypes of the whites and exposing the insecurities of the Negroes. But the progression of values is clear: in order to acknowledge his existence as a man, the hero must first accept the folk legacy of his people; having attained this position, he will discover his identity as an American; but then he must move to the next stage, which expresses the universal values of humanity. The progression is from folk to national and finally international values.

But everything depends on the identification of the folk culture as rich and sufficiently sophisticated to pass the test of the self-appointed culture which judges it to be innately inferior. In order to satisfy these demands, Ellison must first establish the legitimacy of black folk tradition, and his argument runs along lines already familiar to us. The anterior folklore of the Negro (like all folklore) is not simpleminded or barbaric but operates on a level very close to that of formal art. The central question can be resolved in terms of the richness of folk diction, and Ellison gives us several scenes which make the point well. After the narrator arrives in New York he encounters a junk man one morning singing a blues as he pushes his cart along: "She's got feet like a monkey/Legs like a frog—Lawd, Lawd!/But when she starts to loving me/I holler Whoooo, God-dog!/Cause I loves my baabay,/Better than I do myself. . . ." The junk man asks the narrator if he's "got the dog," and the narrator plays "The Arkansas Traveler," pretending he doesn't understand the reference:

> I laughed nervously and stepped back. He watched me out of shrewd eyes. "Oh, goddog, daddy-o," he said with a sudden bluster, "who got the damn dog? Now I know you from down home, how come you trying to act like you never heard that before! Hell, ain't nobody out here this morning but us colored—why you trying to deny me?"

The narrator is uncomfortable in the face of this attempt to make him acknowledge his country background, but he cannot resist the junk man's spiel and his relish for language:

> "Well, daddy-o, it's been good talking with a youngster from the old country but I got to leave you now. This here's one of them good ole downhill streets. I can coast a while and won't be worn out at the end of the day. . . . I thought you was trying to deny me at first, but now I be pretty glad to see you . . ."
> "I hope so," I said. "And you take it easy."
> "Oh, I'll do that. All it takes to get along in this here man's town

is a little shit, grit, and motherwit. And man, I was bawn with all three. In fact, I'maseventhsonofaseventhsonbawnwithacauloverboth eyesandraisedonblackcatboneshighjohntheconquerorandgreasygreens —" he spieled with twinkling eyes, his lips working rapidly. "You dig me, daddy?"

"You're going too fast," I said, beginning to laugh.

"Okay, I'm slowing down. I'll verse you but I won't curse you— my name is Peter Wheatstraw, I'm the Devil's only son-in-law, so roll 'em. You a southern boy, ain't you?" he said, with his head to one side like a bear's.

"Yes," I said.

"Well, git with it! My name's Blue and I'm coming at you with a pitchfork. Fe Fi Fo Fum. Who wants to shoot the devil one, Lord God Stingeroy!"

He had me grinning despite myself. I liked his words though I didn't know the answer. I'd known the stuff from childhood, but had forgotten it; had learned it back of school. . . .

This is only one of several scenes in which the issues of identity, name, and black tradition are brought together. (Joyce has a similar motif in *A Portrait of the Artist* in which a play of language is associated with Stephen's name and relationship to Ireland.) Ellison's nameless narrator is prodded by the junk man to acknowledge his roots as a Southern Negro and though he has been trained to look down his nose at the country people and their culture, he has nevertheless intimations that there is something rich and valuable in their expression. The combination of blues and folk speech appears in several other sequences where the same point is made.

The Jim Trueblood episode, which is one of the best drawn scenes (and to judge from the critics, one of the most problematical) moves along similar lines. The narrator is ordered by one of the white trustees to show him the countryside, and by mistake they arrive at Trueblood's. Mr. Norton is a New Englander who represents the legacy of abolitionism and there are several pointed references to Emerson— "I am a New Englander," Mr. Norton says, "like Emerson. You must learn about him, for he was important to your people. He had a hand in your destiny." Ellison is reacting against the white liberal's patronizing attitude toward the Negro and, as in a later scene involving a young man actually named Emerson, the tone is ironic and pejorative. At the same time, Mr. Norton becomes nostalgic over the memory of his dead daughter, for whom he had an unnatural affection. All this is foreshadowing for the interview with Trueblood, a sharecropper "who told the old stories with a sense of humor and magic that made them come alive. He was also a good tenor singer, and sometimes when special guests visited the school he was brought up along with members of a country quartet to sing what the officials called 'their primitive spirituals' when we assembled in the chapel on Sunday evenings." Ellison's handling of this situation reveals how well he can utilize the materials of folk tradition to expose the full range of their ideological and technical meaning. To begin with, it gives him a chance to undercut the conventional image of the Negro folk character whose major reference for most readers is the kindly Uncle Remus. Norton is ready to receive the impression of a fascinating spinner of tales in the quaint and curious diction of the country folk. What he gets is Trueblood's devastatingly effective recital of incest. Norton reveals the basis for his own interest in the story when he comments, " 'You did and are unharmed!' . . . his blue eyes blazing into the black face with something like envy and indignation." This leads into a little dialogue that employs the strategy of "The Arkansas Traveler":

> "You have looked upon chaos and are not destroyed!"
> "No suh! I feels all right."
> "You do? You feel no inner turmoil, no need to cast out the offending eye?"
> "Suh?"
> "Answer me!"
> "I'm all right suh," Trueblood said uneasily. "My eyes is all right too. And when I feels po'ly in my gut I takes a little soda and it goes away."

The contrast between Norton's stilted diction and Trueblood's folk speech (which is one of the technical achievements of "The Arkansas Traveler" motif) works as well as ever. Ellison has pointed out that the "Negro stereotype is really an image of the unorganized, irrational forces of American life, forces through which, by projecting them in forms of an easily dominated minority, the white individual seeks to be at home in the vast unknown world of America. Perhaps the object of the stereotype is not so much to crush the Negro as to console the white man." It is just this kind of psychological projection that the Trueblood incident illustrates, and it accounts for the compulsion Norton has to hear the tale to the end, relishing every tabooed nuance that Trueblood narrates.

Having punctured the stereotype of the kindly folk character, Ellison pursues the implications of the scene. Like many of Ellison's characters, Trueblood's name carries much of the meaning. Incest is literally being true to one's blood and though Trueblood does not know it, the practice is an ancient and often honorable one, reserved indeed for the aristocracy. It is, in short, an old folkway and Ellison can thereby indicate his rejection of the sentimental notion that folklore will reveal the naiveté and innocence of the common people. The white trustee anticipates a version of pastoral innocence and agrarian antisepsis, quite unaware that for the Negro, pastoral would carry major associations with the horror and brutality of slavery. (Ellison clearly identifies Emerson with just such a simpleminded optimism, although as I have noted earlier, Emerson occasionally recognized that the reliance on folk diction might dredge up some materials that would shock genteel society.) In another more fundamental sense, however, Jim is true to his blood as a man, that is, he experiences the possibility of sin which inheres in the human condition. (Trueblood's dream in the midst of his sexual relations with his daughter invokes images suggesting the fires of hell.) What counts most heavily is Trueblood's reaction after his sin—and after he barely manages to escape the wrath of his wife. (It is true that sex figures prominently in certain areas of Negro folklore, but that should not lead to the dangerous and erroneous conception that Negroes are generally promiscuous—a point made by Trueblood's wife with an axblade!) The old man is rejected by his family, his preacher, and the Negro community but the whites take a great interest in him, encouraging him to tell the story over and over again. Finally, he is forced back on his own resources:

> I leaves tryin' to pray, but I can't. I thinks and thinks until I thinks my brain go'n bust, 'bout how I'm guilty and how I ain't guilty. I don't eat nothin' and I don't drink nothin' and cain't sleep at night. Finally, one night, way early in the mornin', I looks up and sees the stars and starts singin'. I don't know what it was, some kinda church song, I guess. All I know is I *ends up* singin' the blues. I sings me some blues that night ain't never been sang before, and while I'm singin' them blues I makes up my mind that I ain't nobody but myself and ain't nothin' I can do but let whatever is gonna happen happen. I made up my mind that I was goin' back home and face Kate; yeah, and face Matty Lou too.

It will take the rest of the book for Ellison's hero to learn the lesson, but ultimately he comes to the same understanding that "a man ain't nothin' but a man." Unlike Norton, who represses the knowledge of his deep instinct, Trueblood owns up to his sin—it is another sense in which his name is symbolic. But it is important to emphasize that the catharsis occurs through a creative act which Ellison accurately relates to a black folk tradition, the blues. As much as the spirituals, the blues is susceptible of ideological interpretation, though its definition was much later in coming. Yet the form easily takes on esthetic, political, and historical meanings. As one of the major forms of black music, the blues has defined a central tradition in American music at large. The tonality comes from an indeterminacy in several crucial intervals of the scale, the third, fifth, or seventh degrees, which are the so-called blues notes. But actually something more complicated is involved and this is compounded by the fact that one of the characteristics of Negro folk music is that in performance it sounds very different from what any notation can describe. (This is true of all music, but it seems unusually so in black styles which depend on highly complex vocal effects and extensive ornamentation.) The sources of these effects are still not entirely known; some are clearly African, but the "blue notes" themselves do not seem to have African sources.

Although the form is often described as three lines in a twelve bar framework, there is in fact almost an unlimited number of variations possible, with a strong tendency toward improvisation in most authentic performances. But blues suggests sadness, an awareness of trouble or a general lament, and that meaning of the term goes back to Elizabethan usage. The poetry of the blues reveals the ability of the folk to create striking and impressive imagery and in this case it exposes the remarkable range of black folk expression. The themes are often love, death, the sense of loss and at the same time a hope for release and fulfillment. The imagery is often frankly sexual but in highly metaphorical terms which contribute a joy in language and the possibility for a witty humor based on *double-entendre*. Ellison's definition of the blues expresses succinctly and effectively the ideological implications of the form: "the blues is an impulse to keep the painful details and episodes of a brutal experience alive in one's aching consciousness, to finger its jagged grain, and to transcend it, not by the consolation of philosophy but by squeezing from it a near-tragic, near-comic lyricism. As a form, the blues is an autobiographical chronicle of personal catastrophe expressed lyrically." We can see how far this is from earlier conceptions of black music as an expression of hopelessness and chaos. What emerges is an artistic form that makes possible the catharsis we usually associate with tragedy. Ellison pointedly emphasizes that the blues does not skirt the painful facts of human experience, but works through them to an artistic transcendence. We have already seen that this is the formula of Emerson's prescription for achieving the epiphanic moment—to work through the natural fact in order to express the spiritual truth that underlies it. But this similarity is less important than the fact that Ellison recognizes both the force of folk tradition and its close relationship to a sophisticated literary expression. Inevitably such an approach will move against the idea of isolated literary genres (such as tragedy) and in the direction of those mixed modes which seem to define American literary tendencies. The blues is not the "power of positive thinking" but a transformation of catastrophe through the agency of art. This esthetic, like Emerson's, will not allow a poetry of abstract generalization, for the "jagged grain" is valued in its own terms—it is roughly comparable to Emerson's natural facts which make it possible for the low but vital levels of diction to make themselves felt. And because of its close association with black folk culture, it is an esthetic which will also resist a movement toward expression for its own sake. There is, in short, that same balance of natural facts and spiritual truths which pervades a good deal of the literature in America that has been influenced by the Emerson-Whitman tradition.

This is precisely what Trueblood accomplishes with his blues. But Ellison extends this possibility to jazz as well, for if, on the one hand, the blues is a stage forward from earlier black musical expression (work songs, field cries, and spirituals) it is also a major link with jazz; and Ellison's use of jazz as a literary theme is one of his most impressive accomplishments. He raises the issue first in the Prologue, after a reference that comes close to reproducing Emerson's transparent eyeball image: "Nor is my invisibility exactly a matter of a bio-chemical accident to my epidermis. That invisibility to which I refer occurs because of a peculiar disposition of the eyes of those with whom I come in contact. A matter of the construction of their *inner* eyes, those eyes with which they look through their physical eyes upon reality." The mass of men are blind to the spiritual truths, and Ellison's narrator explains that "without light I am not only invisible, but formless as well; and to be unaware of one's form is to live a death." To be free is a function of the awareness of form, that is to say, it is closely related to the creative act, and the analogue of that combination is best defined by jazz: "I'd like to hear five recordings of Louis Armstrong playing and singing 'What Did I Do to Be so Black and Blue'—all at the same time. . . . Perhaps I like Louis because he's made poetry out of being invisible. I think it must be because he's unaware that he *is* invisible. And my own grasp of invisibility aids me to understand his music. . . . Invisibility, let me explain, gives one a slightly different sense of time, you're never quite on the beat. Sometimes you're ahead and sometimes behind. Instead of the swift imperceptible flowing of time, you are aware of its nodes, those points where time stands still or from which it leaps ahead. And you slip into the breaks and look around. That's what you hear vaguely in

Louis' music." Appropriately it is a jazz performance of a blues that the narrator responds to and it is not accidental that the selection has strong social overtones. Ellison's knowledge of the sources of jazz helps him to pinpoint the meaning of Armstrong's music. He knows, for example, that Louis plays cornet (later trumpet), an instrument associated with military bands and that the marching band was one of the musical traditions absorbed and adapted by early New Orleans jazz groups. What Armstrong does with the military tradition is related to what he makes of his invisibility: he bends the inflexible lockstep militarism into a lyrical sound as he turns the condition of invisibility into poetry. It is an affirmation of the ability to overcome oppression through the creation of art and it is another example of Ellison's tendency to associate the idea of freedom with the awareness of form.

In more positive terms, jazz provides one with a new sense of time; again it is not the rhythm of a military march in which everyone must be in step; for despite the regular pulsing beat of a jazz band, there is always the offbeat, or offbeats, which are characteristic of jazz style. Even the drummer, who establishes the fundamental beat, will be more valued if he pushes it a bit, and the instrumentalists will take their solos either slightly behind or ahead of the other musicians. (The ultimate source of this is in black folk tradition where the leader and chorus patterns are strong, but overlapping of the relationship between the two is a standard device—it is what one critic has called "overlapping antiphony.") Instead of a mechanical rhythm, then, jazz demands an awareness of the nodes, those moments within the heart of pulsation which are static or which provide the occasion for a leap to another level of rhythmic awareness. This is an effective description of those essential qualities of jazz syncopation which are difficult to notate but which we recognize as fundamental to the jazz performance. But the rhythmic awareness that Ellison is concerned with also provides an analogy to the recognition of spiritual truths, the opening of the inner eye. The musician slips into the breaks and looks around; he enters into the center of meaning and creates his own statement, which is precisely what the jazz soloist must do. Ellison puts this also in terms of "The Arkansas Traveler" motif. The narrator describes a prize fight between a professional boxer and a yokel: "The fighter was swift and amazingly scientific. His body was one violent flow of rapid rhythmic action. He hit the yokel a hundred times while the yokel, rolling about in the gale of boxing gloves, struck one blow and knocked science, speed and footwork as cold as the well-digger's posterior. The smart money hit the canvas. The long shot got the nod. The yokel had simply stepped inside of his opponent's sense of time." This is precisely what the Squatter does, and in both cases, the opponent never knows what hit him.

The difference between Armstrong and the narrator is important. Louis is not aware of his invisibility because he is positively and deeply associated with the cultural sources of his art. For if jazz provides an outlet for individual expression it also demands an allegiance to the group as well, and Ellison employs this circumstance thematically as a way of defining the relationship of the individual to his society, thus raising the issue from a purely esthetic to a political level as well. It seems to me the best explanation for the denouement of the book in which the narrator affirms his resolve to emerge from underground: "I'm shaking off the old skin, and I'll leave it here in the hole. I'm coming out, no less invisible without it, but coming out nevertheless. And I suppose it's damn well time. Even hibernation can be overdone, come to think of it. Perhaps that's my greatest social crime, I've over-stayed my hibernation, since there's a possibility that even an invisible man has a socially responsible role to play." Louis Armstrong figures prominently in the final decision: "With Louis Armstrong one half of me says, 'Open the window and let the foul air out,' while the other says, 'It was good green corn before the harvest.' Of course Louis was kidding, *he* wouldn't have thrown old Bad Air out, because it would have broken up the music and the dance, when it was the good music that came from the bell of old Bad Air's horn that counted." This is another formulation of Ellison's definition of blues, that transformation of brutal experience into the language of art—the bad air transmitted through Louis' horn becomes the remarkable achievement that we call jazz. And if one part of it is foul, another reflects the green corn, the folk roots of jazz itself. (Foul air is reminiscent of a Jelly Roll Morton tune, "Buddy Bolden's Blues," which is based on the theme of expelling ugly and obnoxious characters; the green corn reference may be to any number of Southern folksongs which use the expression, in dance or play-party tunes, as an image of vitality.)

Ellison reveals his relationship to the folk ideology that I have con-sidered earlier in his awareness that the individual talent draws on the well of tradition from which the art form is derived. This is handled in-directly in the novel, though it counts heavily in the narrator's sense of social responsibility. Ellison develops the idea, however, in one of his essays in *Shadow and Act* where he explains what jazz has meant to him as an artist: "Now, I had learned from the jazz musicians I had known as a boy in Oklahoma City something of the discipline and de-votion to his art required of the artist. . . . These jazzmen, many of them now world famous, lived for and with music intensely. Their driving motivation was neither money or fame, but the will to achieve the most eloquent expression of idea-emotions through the technical mastery of their instruments (which, incidentally, some of them wore as a priest wears the cross) and the give and take, the subtle rhythmical shaping and blending of idea, tone and imagination demanded of group improvisation. The delicate balance struck between strong individual personality and the group during those early jam sessions was a marvel of social organization. I had learned too that the end of all this discipline and technical mastery was the desire to express an affirmative way of life through its musical tradition and this tradition insisted that each artist achieve his creativity within its frame. He must learn the best of the past, and add it to his personal vision. Life could be harsh, loud and wrong if it wished, but they lived it fully, and when they expressed their attitude toward the world it was with a fluid style that reduced the chaos of living to form." This is the antithesis of the earlier attitude toward jazz as the very apex of confusion, but it is also important to note that Ellison's affirmation enables him to solve problems usually considered insoluble by the American writer. In black folklore and the music which issued from it, Ellison finds his sense of the past, and also the basis for his commitment to technical and artistic competence. But the technical accomplishment of the jazz musician is never strictly an individual phenomenon, however much improvisation and personal vision are valued. For underlying it is the folk tradition from which it emerged and hence, as Herder had pointed out, there is a communal base which the folk themselves provided as a legacy to the individual artist. That delicate balance which Ellison describes between the individual and the group in a jam session becomes as well a description of what the society as a whole might be. The political implications of Ellison's folk ideology begin to emerge as inevitably as in the approaches of the writers I have discussed earlier. For jazz is a uniquely American expression and when we understand it as Ellison does, it encompasses just that sense of individualism directed toward communal concerns which we have already encountered in Emerson and Whitman. The metaphor of the jazzman illustrates the relationship better than any analogy we have seen to this point. Jazz values improvisation, personal vision, an assault on the conventional modes of musical expression, but it will not allow the individual to forget what he owes to tradition—not the tradition of a great man, but the legacy shaped by a whole people. It is precisely what folk ideologues have always argued: the authentic sources of a nation's culture lie in the lower levels and if they are developed sensitively, not only the poet speaks but his nation also finds its expression.

Hence the narrator of *Invisible Man* is finally able to unravel the meaning of his grandfather's advice: "I want you to overcome 'em with yeses, undermine 'em with grins, agree 'em to death and destruction, let 'em swoller you till they vomit or bust open." At first he takes this to mean accepting the values of the white world, playing the good Negro, all the while making the most of his opportunities for himself. But ultimately he understands that the grandfather's plea for affirmation was toward something else: "Could he have meant—hell he *must* have meant the principle, that we were to affirm the principle on which the country was built and not the men, or at least not the men who did the violence. Did he mean say 'yes' because he knew that the principle was greater than the men, greater than the numbers and the vicious power and all the methods used to corrupt its name? Did he mean to affirm the principle, which they themselves dreamed into being out of the chaos and darkness of the feudal past, and which they had violated and compromised to the point of absurdity even in their own corrupt minds? Or did he mean that we had to take the responsibility for all of it, for the men as well as the principle because no other fitted our needs? Not for the power or for vindication, but because we, with the given circumstances of our origin, could only thus find transcendence?" For all his awareness of evil and his contempt for an easy optimism, the narrator reveals himself to be essentially an Emersonian "yea sayer." He has tried all the versions of the American dream, beginning with the tradition that hard work and prudence will lead to material success. "Though invisible, I am in the great American tradition of tinkers," the narrator explains at the outset. "That makes me kin to Ford, Edison and Franklin. Call me, since I have a theory and a concept, a 'thinker-tinker.' " But what he finally learns is to accept his humanity (as his grandfather and Louis Armstrong always have) and the idea of self-reliance: "But my world has become one of infinite possibilities. What a phrase—still it's a good phrase and a good view of life, and a man shouldn't accept any other; that much I've learned underground. Until some gang succeeds in putting the world in a strait jacket, its definition is possibility. Step outside the narrow borders of what men call reality and you step into chaos—ask Rinehart, he's a master of it—or imagination. That too I've learned in the cellar, and not by deadening my sense of perception; I'm invisible, not blind." This is essentially what one strand of Emerson's thought has come to suggest—that the reality of our life needs to be held constantly to the demands of the American dream; and when it fails to measure up to the standard, it is the individual's responsibility to say so. But Emerson's individualism was balanced by an awareness of national requirements, which would be best expressed esthetically in the creation of a truly

American art. The principle that Ellison's narrator affirms is best defined as nonconformity, but it contains also a commitment to that balance between individualism and communal responsibility which we noted in Whitman's concern with both the "I and the en-masse"; the danger is still that the balance will be tilted in the extreme of either direction: "Now I know that men are different and all life is divided and that only in division is there true health. . . . Whence all this passion toward conformity anyway?—diversity is the word. Let man keep his many parts and you'll have no tyrant states. Why if they follow this conformity business they'll end up forcing me to become white, which is not a color but the lack of one. Must I strive toward colorlessness? But seriously, and without snobbery, think of what the world would lose if that should happen. America is woven of many strands; I would recognize them and let it so remain. It's winner take nothing that is the great truth of our country or of any country. Life is to be lived, not controlled; and humanity is won by continuing to play in face of certain defeat. Our fate is to become one, yet many—This is not prophecy but description."

The character who symbolizes the idea of possibilities as a way of life is Rinehart, ideologically the most important figure in the book, though dramatically just a sketch. In response to a question about Rinehart, Ellison recalled that the name appeared in one of blues singer Jimmy Rushing's songs and was not a conscious play on Django Rhinehardt, the great jazz guitarist. The line from the blues was haunting, "and as I was thinking of a character who was a master of disguise, of coincidence, this name with its suggestion of inner and outer came to mind. Later I learned that it was a call used by Harvard students when they prepared to riot, a call to chaos. Which is very interesting, because it is not long after Rinehart appears in my novel that the riot breaks out in Harlem. Rinehart is my name for the personification of chaos. He is also intended to represent America and change. He has lived so long with chaos that he knows how to manipulate it. It is the old theme of *The Confidence Man*. He is a figure in a country with no solid or stable past or stable class lines; therefore he is able to move about easily from one to the other." The reference to Melville is interesting because it seems to me that stylistically Ellison is closer to him than any other source, and this seems the more evident if we recall Melville's use of Emerson's esthetic and his insistence on seeing the darker implications of Emerson's political philosophy. But Rinehart's ability to manipulate chaos also suggests that he is a symbol of the artist. He is a Proteus and Ellison himself has made this analogy with the artist: "For the novelist, Proteus stands for both America and the inheritance of illusion through which all men must fight to achieve reality. . . ." Encountering Rinehart in an evangelical mission, the narrator finally understands his function: "I had heard it before but I'd never come so close. Still, could he be all of them: Rine the runner and Rine the gambler and Rine the briber and Rine the lover and Rinehart the Reverend? Could he himself be both rind and heart? What is real anyway? But how could I doubt it? He was a broad man, a man of parts who got around. Rinehart the rounder. It was true as I was true. His world was possibility and he knew it. He was years ahead of me and I was a fool. I must have been crazy and blind. The world in which we lived was without boundaries. A vast seething, hot world of fluidity, and Rine the rascal was at home in it. It was unbelievable, but perhaps only the unbelievable could be believed. Perhaps the truth was always a lie." Yet although Rinehart is closest to the truth he has a major fault; he is in danger of tipping the scales too far in the direction of selfish exploitation of the world's possibilities. He is irresponsible in not acknowledging the communal sources of that artistic power which enables him to master illusion. (It is the analogue of art for art's sake and Ellison is as uncomfortable as Emerson at the prospect.) Rinehart, to recall Cotton Mather's metaphor of the sinner rowing toward heaven, is like a man pulling only one oar; he has forgotten his social responsibilities.

Hence, although Rinehart is attractive, he cannot provide the narrator with a complete world view. And Ellison has resented inferences that his narrator will remain an antihero, simply a version of Dostoievsky's underground man: "The final act of *Invisible Man*," he notes, "is not that of a concealment in darkness in the Anglo-Saxon connotation of the word, but that of a voice issuing its little wisdom out of the substance of its own inwardness—after having undergone a transformation from ranter to writer. . . . And in keeping with the reverse English of the plot, and with the Negro American conception of blackness, his movement vertically downward (not into a 'sewer,' Freud notwithstanding, but into a coal cellar, a source of heat, light, power and through association with the character's motivation, self-perception) is a process of *rising* to an understanding of his human condition." That underground suggests as well the substratum of folk culture upon which an American art can be built, and Ellison's hero plays a variation on the Marxist dictum: "All boundaries down, freedom was not only the recognition of necessity, it was the recognition of possibility."

The narrator will not give up his color because that would mean rejecting as well the heritage of black culture which, as Ellison has argued, is a major contribution to America as well. But the force of black culture (in folklore and jazz) is to remind us of the principle especially appropriate for American development—that the roots of high culture lie in the expression of the common people. Ellison modifies the optimism of Emerson's ideology with his blues formulation; it is what he means by "continuing to play in face of certain defeat"—play refers not just to the game, but also to Louis Armstrong playing his music, though conscious that he is black and blue. What Ellison has in mind in his formulation of equality recalls Herder's conception of the equal validity of incommensurable cultures. The aim is not to make the Negro white, or the white Negro, but to allow for the fullest development of each strand which will ultimately contribute to the definition of a black *and* white America. It is not black nationalism Ellison is after, but American nationalism as the Emerson-Whitman tradition had defined it. For the Negro it means first accepting his folk heritage in order to be an American; then he can acknowledge his status as a man. (Ellison knows that "in the United States when traditions are juxtaposed they tend, regardless of what we do to prevent it, irresistibly to merge," and he adds: "Those who know their native culture and love it unchauvinistically are never lost when encountering the unfamiliar.") Meanwhile the familiar strategy continues to work. It is the seeming barbarian whose level of culture defines the highest values of our civilization, while his language revitalizes our literary expression.

This has been the central motif of this study and Ellison has defined even more accurately what it has meant for his own career as an artist. The Negro's experience, he noted, "is that of America and the West, and is as rich a body of experience as one can find anywhere. We can view it narrowly as something exotic, folksy, or 'low-down,' or we may identify ourselves with it and recognize it as an important segment of the larger American experience—not lying at the bottom of it, but intertwined, diffused in its very texture." The irony is that Americans at large still need to be convinced that it is so.

Epilogue

The Poetry of Rock:
Folk Tradition and
the Individual Talent

ONE DOESN'T ordinarily think of T. S. Eliot as a folk poet. Yet in some respects Eliot has responded to folk tradition in a way characteristic of the writers I have been discussing. Despite Eliot's dodging behind more respectable labels for the source of his work and some of his esthetic preferences, his interest in "anthropology" was really a response to the many strands of folk tradition that Sir James Frazer collected in the impressive and often inaccurate volumes of *The Golden Bough*. (As Theodor H. Gaster has pointed out, aside from the fact that a good many of his major views were based on inaccurate accounts assembled by untrained observers, Frazer failed "persistently to distinguish between the *savage* and the *primitive*, so that on closer analysis many of his examples turn out to be irrelevant or even misleading."[1]) Similarly, Eliot's interest in Jessie L. Weston's study of the relationships between pagan religion and Christian ritual (*From Ritual to Romance*) led him squarely to an area where folklore is at least one of the central traditions under consideration, despite Miss Weston's insistence that her real concern was comparative religion. It's also worth recalling Eliot's appropriation of Mallarmé's dictum which describes the function of the poet: *"donner un sens plus pur aux mots de la tribu."* Eliot's reputation as a scholarly, obscure poet overshadows the obvious inferences to be drawn from this definition. But if we poke around the edges of Eliot's public image it is not difficult to catch the connotations of Mallarmé's formulation. It is, I suggest, a reference to the folk bard, who traditionally has the responsibility for raising the idiom of the people to its highest level, thus preserving the sense of the past and clarifying the meaning of the present for the mass of men in a society. It is significant that Eliot translates *mots* as "dialect," for he surely understood the association of that word with "substandard," regional or colloquial speech. Indeed he says as much in *The Use of Poetry and the Use of Criticism:* "The people which ceases to produce literature ceases to move in thought and sensibility. The poetry of a people takes its life from the people's speech and in turn gives life to it; and represents its highest point of consciousness, its greatest power and its most delicate sensibility."[2]

Later in the same book Eliot discusses the question of obscurity in modern poetry: "To return to the question of obscurity: when all exceptions have been made, and after admitting the possible existence of minor 'difficult' poets whose public must always be small, I believe that the poet naturally prefers to write for as large and miscellaneous an audience as possible, and that it is the half-educated and ill-educated, rather than the uneducated who stand in his way; I myself should like an audience which could neither read nor write. The most useful poetry, socially, would be one which could cut across all the present stratifications of public taste—stratifications which are perhaps a sign of social disintegration."

Eliot makes it clear that "social usefulness" cannot mean that poetry should be a substitute for some other discipline such as sociology, economics, or theology; the poet should not "do anything but write poetry, poetry not defined in terms of something else." Consequently, although Eliot rejects the idea of "pure poetry" he recognizes the kernel of truth in the art-for-art's-sake esthetic which emphasizes "the error of the poet's trying to do other people's work." Yet the central implications of Eliot's arguments led him to a concern with the precarious balance between the poet's individual achievement and the responsibility to the communal sources of which he is both the inheritor and the guardian. His interest in folk tradition (and folk speech) is often a reflection of nostalgia for a period in human development when the poet had a precise social function acknowledged by "the tribe"—that audience which could neither read nor write; it looks back to a primitive era before social stratification split society into an uneasy collection of social and intellectual classes, which is why Eliot refers to the phenomenon as "perhaps a sign of social disintegration." Eliot is so troubled by this alienation of the poet from his audience that he suggests, "From one point of view, the poet aspires to the condition of the music-hall comedian. Being incapable of altering his wares to suit a prevailing taste, if there be any, he naturally desires a state of society in which they may become popular, and in which his own talents will be put to the best use." That comment appears at the beginning of *The Use of Poetry*. At the end he returns to a similar idea. The poet would like to be "something of a popular entertainer. . . . He would like to convey the pleasures of poetry, not only to a large audience, but to larger groups of people collectively"; and this, he says, might "give an immediate compensation for the pains of turning blood into ink." No poet can be certain he has not "wasted his time and messed up his life for nothing. All the better then, if he could have the satisfaction of having a part to play in society as worthy as that of the music-hall comedian."

The closest any poet can come to achieving rapport with a large audience, Eliot thought, was in the theater. And while this was true at various times in the past (Shakespeare is the example Eliot cites), the popular music of the 1960's and beyond represents a similar occurrence, one, moreover, which has close connections with the traditions that have interested me in this study. I think it is worth discussing the renaissance of popular song within the framework of Eliot's ideas, especially within the context of his essay, "Tradition and the Individual Talent."[3] It is Eliot who has chided us for emphasizing the esoteric elements in a poet's work, ignoring the fact that often "the most individual parts of his work may be those in which the dead poets, his ancestors, assert their immortality most vigorously." We need to invoke the historical sense, Eliot suggests, "which compels a man to write not merely with his generation in his bones, but with a feeling that the whole of the literature of Europe from Homer and within it the whole of the literature of his own country has a simultaneous existence and composes a simultaneous order." That, according to Eliot, is what makes a poet aware of his relationship to the past as well as the present and the "timeless" in addition. This is another instance of Eliot's reliance on folklore in the formulation of a crucial esthetic principle. For that sense of the past which, according to Eliot, the modern poet must learn "by great labour," is the natural inheritance of the folk poet, though of course the folk bard will not approach the cosmopolitanism that Eliot proposes.

I am well aware that Eliot is often far removed from this esthetic in his own work and that his expatriation led him to underplay "the literature of his own country" while emphasizing "the whole of the literature of Europe" and even the Orient. It is also true that we are not used to talking about popular music in terms of esthetics; indeed until the advent of "rock" music, few scholars have talked about popular music at all. But I think that an examination of the rock scene will provide us with an opportunity for clarifying some additional relationships between folklore, popular music, and formal literature. In particular, I want to point out the continuing influence of Herderian folk ideology, Emerson's symbolist esthetic, and the central force of black musical styles.

I am interested in rock music because it is apparent that some unusually interesting things are happening in the words and music of the popular songs that began to appear at the beginning of the decade of the sixties. In fact, some critics have suggested that Bob Dylan is the great poet of the twentieth century, and though that is hardly the case, Dylan and some of his contemporaries are in that enviable position that Eliot described: like the music-hall comedians, they have found a broad audience and they are having a significant impact on it. But among other things, they are proving the accuracy of what has often sounded like a typically naive Emersonian dictum. Not only the poets, Emerson noted, but all men are fascinated by symbols: "The inwardness and mystery of its attachment drive men of every class to the use of emblems. . . . The people fancy that they hate poetry, and they are all poets and mystics." The best of the rock songwriters have destroyed the Tin Pan Alley hack tradition and replaced it with a symbolist technique which is often undisciplined and occasionally incomprehensible but which has close connections with a main line of American literary development.

Dylan is a good example of how some of these young writers have responded to the traditional materials available to them. He began as a disciple (almost a reincarnation) of Woody Guthrie, the writer-singer who emerged as a major figure in the folksong "revival" of the fifties, a phenomenon sparked by such groups as the Weavers. By 1949 the latter had managed to get one of Huddie Ledbetter's songs, "Good Night, Irene," to the top of the hit parade. (Ironically, both Leadbelly and John Lomax had died the year before.) After that it was open season on folk materials, although the style of the songs being exploited by most groups was contained within the traditions of commercial music. These were characterized by lush orchestral arrangements of folk tunes, expurgation of suggestive texts, and unskilled imitations of traditional black and white vocal styles. (The last line of "Good Night, Irene" was originally, "I'll *get* you in my dreams"; it was changed to "I'll *see* you in my dreams," and eventually even Leadbelly himself sang it that way!) Guthrie, it will be recalled, was a traditional performer and prolific songwriter who had been discovered by the Lomaxes, and many of his songs became standards in the repertoire of folk-oriented groups. His Whitmanesque paean to America, "This Land Is Your Land," was adopted as the theme song for the whole folksong movement. The more important point is that for the first time in our history the great variety of American folksong was made available to mass audiences. As Pete Seeger, an old friend of Guthrie's and one of the original members of the Weavers, has pointed out, Guthrie's songs were honest; they said things that needed to be said about the lives of outcast and exploited people. They emphasized, in short, what I have described as the Herderian folk ideology, asserting the dignity of the common people, concentrating on such issues as peace and democracy, championing the rights of strikers, migrant workers, and the poor folk (black and white) of the South. At the same time, Guthrie associated himself with left-wing causes and organizations; during the McCarthy era Guthrie, like Seeger himself and countless others, was effectively blacklisted by the mass media.

But as Seeger notes, Guthrie "had a deep respect for the ballad form.

He knew enough about other song forms to choose among many others, but he felt that the old four-line stanza, which told a story and slowly unfolded a moral, was as good as any he could use."[4] We should recall here Whitman's refusal to write literary ballads. He seemed to understand that a literal adherence to Herder's esthetic often led to a dead end in which the poet simply imitated the surface forms of folk styles. In fact, Goethe, who was at first attracted to Herder's ideology, later rejected the approach on just such grounds. American writers avoided that pitfall, as we have seen, by combining Herder's ideology with Emerson's sophisticated insights into the nature of symbolism. The result, as we have seen in Whitman, is a formal style which reflects folk tradition but is not limited by its shortcomings. Significantly, Guthrie once wrote to Seeger, "I must remember to steer clear of Walt Whitman's swimmy waters." Until he was incapacitated by a long, terminal illness, Guthrie developed his talents closely within the framework of the folk tradition that he inherited from his Oklahoma background.

"Pastures of Plenty," one of the many songs Guthrie wrote about the plight of migrant workers, is a good example of his style at its best:

It's a mighty hard row that my poor hands has hoed,
These poor feet has travelled a hot dusty road.
Out of your dustbowl and westward we rolled,
Well, your deserts was hot and your mountains was cold.

I work in your orchards of peaches and prunes,
I sleep on the ground 'neath the light of your moon.
On the edge of your cities you'll see us and then,
We come with the dust and we go with the wind.

California, Arizona I make all your crops,
Then it's north up to Oregon to gather your hops.
Dig the beets from your ground, cut the grapes from your vines,
To set on your table your light sparkling wines.

Green pastures of plenty from dry desert ground,
From the Grand Coulee Dam where the waters run down;
Every state in this union us migrants has been—
We'll work in this fight and we'll fight till we win.

It's always we ramble that river and I.
All along your green valleys I'll work till I die;
My land I'll defend with my life if needs be,
For my pastures of plenty must always be free.

Guthrie's diction is vernacular, the images are precise, effective, and often reminiscent of older lines that have appeared in traditional songs on similar themes. "A hard row to hoe" is a folk expression still used to define the difficult straits of poor farmers. But Guthrie has also emphasized the westward pull that has characterized American development and has added his commitment to such internal improvements as the Coulee Dam. Although the image of the migrant suggests mobility and a freedom which comes from not being tied down to conventional employment (an attitude often symbolized by the hobo's Thoreauvian disdain for material possessions), there is also an agrarian association with the land. The vague reference to a fight alludes to the repeated but unsuccessful attempts to organize farm workers and provide them with the benefits gained by other segments of the labor force. But the most significant ideological implication is that the migrant, though outcast and embattled, reminds the society at large of its commitment to freedom and the dignity of the common man. It is precisely what the Lomaxes had identified as the significant theme in American folksong—a theme they had found most clearly expressed in the songs that emanated from black culture. Guthrie wants to make his point clearly and in order to do so he avoids complicated symbolism. (The tune Guthrie used for "Pastures of Plenty" follows closely an American murder ballad, "Pretty Polly.")

Dylan became a major innovator by immersing himself in Whitman's "swimmy waters." That is, he initiated the movement toward an Emersonian esthetic, adapting the most sophisticated verse techniques to a basically folk style, thus reproducing on the level of popular song what had been a major literary approach since Whitman. The resulting style is sometimes called folk-rock and is exemplified in the work of Dylan, Simon and Garfunkel, and a great many imitators. Folk-rock relies heavily on a *Waste Land* imagery that attempts to expose the alienation and absurdity of modern civilization. (Paul Simon has a characteristic line in his song, "The Sounds of Silence": "The words of the prophets are written on subway walls, tenement halls. . . .") Dylan's song, "A Hard Rain's A Gonna Fall," begins with lines that recall the old ballad, "Lord Randall"; but in place of the dramatic narrative one expects in ballad tradition, Dylan provides a catalogue of apocalyptic images:

> Oh, where have you been, my blue-eyed son?
> Oh, where have you been, my darling young one?
>
> I've stumbled on the side of twelve misty mountains,
> I've walked and I've crawled on six crooked highways,
> I've stepped in the middle of seven sad forests,

I've been out in front of a dozen dead oceans,
I've been ten thousand miles in the mouth of a graveyard,
And it's a hard, and it's a hard, it's a hard, and it's a hard,
And it's a hard rain's a gonna fall.*

This is the mode Dylan has continued to develop, and although many of his efforts are what pop musicians call "message songs," the elements of protest are clearly subordinated to the exercise of a complex imagery which is notably different from the straightforward affirmations of Guthrie's songs.[5]

Dylan's defection from the Guthrie style was attacked furiously by folk music purists, most of whom were unaware of Constance Rourke's assertion that American folk music has never been "ethnic" in a European sense of the term. The greatest cries arose as a consequence of Dylan's use of amplified instruments for backgrounds in place of a setting limited to a solo singer accompanying himself on acoustic guitar. Here also Dylan was defining a new relationship between the contemporary songwriter and the traditions available to him. (Country-western musicians have been using amplified instruments for many years.) Folk-rock quickly developed in a number of directions characterized by such labels as "soft rock," "hard rock," and "acid rock"; these are often impressionistic terms, but they signify the discovery by young musicians of materials and techniques adapted from folk, jazz, pop, country-western, and even chamber and concert music. The approach of major innovative groups, however, has followed closely the poetic experiments of Dylan. It is indeed a new approach for popular music, but it also represents an attitude that has deep roots in our literary history.

One of the main effects of popular music, on the other hand, has been to mask the close connections between black and white styles. Beginning with the mixing of styles during the Great Awakening of the eighteenth-century and down to the present time, black vocal and instrumental styles have periodically been infused into our folk and popular traditions; but white Americans have generally known only the diluted versions of the music as it came to them through the mass media. Rock music has confirmed the major influence of black styles on our popular music, recalling also the Lomaxes' assertion that it was "the Negroes who, in our opinion, have made the important and original contribution to American folksong." In the history of jazz, black musicians have been the innovators, from Jelly Roll Morton to Theolonious Monk; rock music is the most recent instance of the expropriation by whites of a tradition pioneered by blacks. As Eldridge Cleaver has pointed out in *Soul on Ice*, white jazz musicians "were famous for going to Harlem and other Negro cultural centers literally to steal the black man's music, carrying it back across the color line in the Great White World and passing off the watered-down loot as their own original creations."[6] The less complex popular music of city blacks, Cleaver notes, "which was known as Rhythm and Blues before the whites appropriated and distilled it into the product they called Rock 'n Roll—is the basic ingredient, the core of the gaudy, cacophonous hymns" of the Beatles, who have attempted to present what Cleaver calls "soul by proxy" to their avid fans. (To appreciate the delicious irony of Cleaver's comment, one has to recall how regularly "cacophonous" has appeared as an epithet describing jazz and other black musical styles.)

Although Cleaver is furious at this latest example of cultural piracy, he notes that black music may nevertheless provide the "saving link, the bridge between man's biology and man's machines." That was Chubby Checker's mission, says Cleaver, "bearing the Twist as *good news,* to teach the whites, whom history had taught to forget, how to shake their asses again." It is a gospel, we can all testify, that has been widely accepted. Cleaver's argument is that modern man needs to be made whole, taught to live with his body as well as his mind; in fact it is Cleaver's solution to the problem which Eliot has defined as the "dissociation of sensibility." What is more germane to my discussion is the obviously Herderian framework of Cleaver's assertion. In a world increasingly automated, mechanized, and bodiless, man's "need for affirmation of his biology" becomes crucial. "This great mass hunger," Cleaver continues, "which transcends national or racial boundaries, recoils from the subtle subversions of the mechanical environment which modern technology is creating faster than man, with his present savage relationship to his fellow man, is able to receive and assimilate." This is the central contradiction of our time and it is within this context that "America's attempt to unite its Mind with its Body, to save its soul, is taking place." This is a good gloss on the meaning of "soul," which refers to the quality and the style of black culture and which is offered as a form of therapy for a sick society. The latest version of this process, which as we have seen is a basic component of Herder's folk ideology, seems to Cleaver an agreement in which "the whites have had to turn to the blacks for a clue on how to swing with the Body, while the blacks have had to turn to the whites for the secret of the Mind." Song and dance are the means by which "man purges his soul of the tensions of daily strife and maintains harmony with the universe," and song and dance are precisely the gifts which the blacks have given to American culture. But as in the other instances we have examined, the lower levels of society provide the sources of revitalization.

The rock music of the sixties is not the last stage in a development which I think we can understand best within the framework I have been discussing. The Herderian folk ideology, with its special significance for the American experience; the increasing influence of an Emersonian symbolist esthetic; and the continuing awareness of the central force of black musical styles—all these have combined to release impressive artistic expression both here and abroad. It needs to be pointed out that most pop music is still "pap" music and that the music industry seems capable of vulgarizing every new approach. Many of the young song-writers, like Dylan himself, seem overwhelmed by the poetic resources they are trying to fashion into a new tradition. They are often annoyingly Whitmanesque, surrealist, dadaist, or simply banal; they have not yet found a way to relate comfortably to the black sources that are at the heart of their music (especially the blues) and hence they are often still "black impersonators." (At the same time it should be noted that black performers are beginning to achieve their own recognition in pop music, but sometimes at the cost of their cultural integrity; and there is at least one black singer who has made it as a Nashville country performer who is, on records, indistinguishable from white singers.)

As Eliot has noted, "the bad poet is usually unconscious where he ought to be conscious, and conscious where he ought to be unconscious." But at its best, rock presents a "primitive accumulation" of artistic materials which has had a profound impact on our conception of folk, popular, and formal literary traditions. Although it has just begun to show itself in formal literary traditions, its function at the present time is more sociological than esthetic. (Aside from the fact that it is wedded to song, which is usually a great advantage for poetry, a great deal of rock verse is patently subliterary.) But Cleaver is right when he notes that, "The white youth of today have begun to react to the fact that the 'American way of life' is a fossil of history. What do they care if their baldheaded and crew-cut elders don't dig their caveman mops? They couldn't care less about the old stiffassed honkies who don't like their new dances: Frug, Monkey, Jerk, Swim, Watusi. All they know is that it feels good to swing to way-out body rhythms instead of dragassing across the dance floor like zombies to the dead beat of mind-smothered Mickey Mouse music." The music of the seventies continues to lay bare the waste land qualities of American life while, at the same time, it revives our sensibilities with new vibrations. "The times they are a'changin'," as Dylan has said, and as in any transitional period the main thrust throws us off balance. But we might also recall Emerson's response to the changes he perceived taking place in his own time. "If there is any period one would desire to be born in," he asked, "is it not the age of Revolution; when the old and the new stand side by side and admit of being compared; when the energies of all men are searched by fear and by hope; when the historic glories of the old can be compensated by the rich possibilties of the new era? This time, like all times, is a very good one, if we but know what to do with it." Emerson himself knew well that the richest literary possibilities for a new era needed to be derived from a calculated use of traditional materials; in that way, the voice of the folk would speak through the work of our most accomplished artists.

Appendix

America's Folk Instrument:
The Five-String Banjo

THE ATTEMPT to discover the ultimate origin of most musical instruments is limited not only by the absence of precise information but also by the fact that the physical nature of some (such as the banjo) makes it unlikely that they would survive during any long period of time. Still there is general agreement among those musicologists who have paid attention to it that the banjo flourished in Africa, although it was probably brought there by other peoples. *Grove's Dictionary of Music and Musicians* states that "instruments resembling . . . the banjo have been discovered in various parts of Africa," but adds the comment that "the continent of Asia was originally connected with the continent of Africa by a strip of land" and that "any instrument known in Asia in ancient times would almost certainly be known in Africa through the intermediary of the Egyptians."[1]

Whatever its provenance, however, there is little doubt that the banjo was brought to this country by Negro slaves. One of the earliest references to an instrument like the banjo appears in a poem written by an Englishman in the British West Indies in 1763: "On festal days or when their work is done/ Permit thy slaves to lead the choral dance/ To the wild *banshaw's* melancholy sound."[2] Since many slaves were often "broken in" on plantations in the West Indies before shipment to this country, it seems likely that some kind of acculturation had already taken place in the islands.

In this country the connection between the banjo and Negro slaves was noted by Thomas Jefferson who, in his *Notes on Virginia* (1781), observed of his plantation slaves, "The instrument proper to them is the Banjar, which they brought hither from Africa and which is the original of the guitar, its chords [strings] being precisely the four lower chords of the guitar."[3] Jefferson was wrong in thinking that the banjo was "the original of the guitar." But in addition to this mention of the instrument's name, Jefferson's description is interesting because it indicates that he saw a *four-stringed* instrument and because it tells us something of the tuning. African banjos are constructed of gourds or other similar materials as well as frame drums with a varying number of strings. But mainly because of Jefferson's comment it is often assumed that the banjos made by plantation slaves were four-stringed, gourd instruments. Gilbert Chase states, for example: "It is a pity that Jefferson did not describe the construction of the 'banjar' as it existed in his time. Very likely it was made in the same primitive fashion followed by later generations of Negroes. The seeds were scooped out of a large gourd, and the bowl cut away so as to be level with the handle attached to it. Over the bowl of the gourd a tanned coonskin was tightly stretched, forming a drumhead. Four strings were passed over a bridge placed near the center of the drum and attached to the neck or handle of the instrument."[4]

In view of the importance attached by later writers to Jefferson's comment, it is indeed too bad that he was not more precise. Whether accurate or not, Jefferson's statement is the major source of the idea that the plantation banjo was a gourd instrument with four strings. Since the four lower strings of the guitar are E A d g, one may also assume that the banjar was tuned in fourths, though such a tuning does not appear to have been retained either by four-string or five-string banjo players. And of course although Jefferson was an amateur violinist, we cannot be sure that he reported the tuning accurately. The conjecture is further complicated by the fact that the guitar was in a transitional period during the eighteenth century, moving from a characteristically five-stringed instrument toward the final form which had six. In view of our interest in the invention of the fifth banjo string, it's worth quoting a recent comment by a historian of the guitar: "The 'invention' of the sixth string of the guitar is often attributed to a German instrument-maker, the Weimar luthier August Otto—a claim which is all the more difficult to believe because up to that point [the eighteenth century] the German musical world was otherwise occupied . . . Herr Otto claimed that he and a Dresden conductor first had the idea of adding the low E-string to the guitar, and this claim has been accepted at face value by many subsequent writers. Actually, of course, it was another of those inventions, like the telephone, that occur to different people in different places at the same time. Instrument makers in the Mediterranean countries, with the precedent of the six-course vihuela to fall back on, had been experimenting with six-string guitars for nearly a century."[5]

These questions concerning the construction and tuning of the banjo are not merely academic ones; rather they have become central to the argument that the five-string, frame banjo is a distinctly American development. Proponents of this view assert that the American banjo may be distinguished from its predecessors by the addition of the fifth string (which usually runs halfway up the neck and produces the characteristic ring of the instrument), and the substitution of the frame drum for the gourd as a sound box. John and Alan Lomax were among the first to identify the five-string banjo as an American development, suggesting that its history mirrored the essential character of American folk song, which derives largely from the merging of British and West African folk traditions. In *Folk Song U.S.A.* Alan Lomax stated: "Wherever the minstrel show and its music penetrated in America, it carried along the five-string banjo, which might be said to be America's only original folk instrument. It is related on its mother's side to certain primitive West African stringed instruments; it was raised up by Negro slaves; it was polished and given its fifth string by one Joel Sweeney of North Carolina [sic] in 1840; and strangely, it found its final home, after everyone had grown tired of it, in the lonesome hollers of the Southern mountains. When the mountain fiddlers heard it, they gave up their fiddles, sat down with the contraption and worked on it till they had produced a kind of music that was neither Afro-American, nor minstrel style, nor a transcription of their old tunes, but a peculiar and wonderful mixture of all these." The argument here is that although it originated elsewhere, the banjo underwent sufficient changes in the United States to justify the claim that it is our "only original folk instrument." It was perhaps to bolster this idea (which, as I have tried to show, is typical of the Lomaxes' pioneering attempts to establish the view that America does have a unique folk tradition) that the Sweeney story was propagated.

Joel Walker Sweeney has indeed been widely acknowledged as the "inventor" of the five-string, frame banjo, although the claim is based mainly on the fact that Sweeney and his friends said that he did. Sweeney became popular as a minstrel banjoist in this country as well as in England, advertising himself as the "Celebrated Banjo Player and Negro Melodist." According to Arthur Woodward, Sweeney learned to play the banjo from Negro slaves on the family plantation near Appomatox, Virginia.[6] A contemporary of Sweeney's commented, "I believe there is no doubt that he was the first to put the thumb string on the banjo, the 'chaunter' or 'chanter' we called it then, but I've not heard the word in years." Woodward himself states, "As Joel grew older he became dissatisfied with the gourd shell, and made an instrument of wood with a skin head instead of the more fragile gourd. About the year 1831 he added a fifth or thumb string to this new invention, thus producing the first of a long line of banjos."

As we shall see, Lomax was probably correct in his assertion that the banjo developed uniquely in this country. But there is good reason to question the statement that Sweeney invented either the fifth string or the frame drum. Since it is clear that Sweeney learned what he knew about the banjo from plantation slaves, it is reasonable to assume that he learned about the "chanter" or drone string from them too. And this is all the more likely since the use of a drone string on musical instruments has a long history. Curt Sachs, for example, has pointed out that the Greeks in ancient times probably tuned their lyres "with a high string close to the lowest one of an ascending scale (like the modern banjo). . . ."[7] This characterizes precisely the arrangement of strings on the five-string banjo: the fifth or drone (which is the highest in pitch) is placed next to the lowest pitched string on the instrument. The Indian sitar also has a similarly arranged thumb string. And *Grove's Dictionary* quotes an early work (1688) which describes a banjo-like instrument of Jamaican Negroes as "sometimes made of hollowed timber, covered with parchment or other skin. . . ."[8] In view of these precedents it seems inappropriate to credit Sweeney with having "invented" either the fifth string or the frame drum for the banjo.

As Professor Hans Nathan has demonstrated, however, the white minstrel banjoists have provided us with the only information bearing on plantation instrumental music. As I have already noted, the vogue of minstrelsy represents one of a series of recurring infusions of black instrumental and vocal styles into the mainstream of American folk and popular music. After the civil war, a large number of slave songs were collected, with occasional comments about the vocal styles employed. But very little is known about plantation instrumental music. The basic instrument of the white minstrel was the five-string, frame drum banjo and the music he played, though often filtered through the consciousness of composers like Dan Emmett and Stephen Foster, reflected the characteristic instrumental style of the plantation Negro. Since these tunes and styles were based on oral tradition, it is impossible to know what they actually sounded like. But when the minstrels began to publish banjo method books they included many tunes that were based on black folk styles. From an analysis of the tunes contained in these manuals, Nathan has concluded that "the minstrel banjo style is very similar to what the slaves played on their banjos and fiddles. Some of the tunes may very well be the originals or close imitations of them. This would be a significant fact because no other record of early instrumental plantation music is left to us."[9] The slaves sang the Irish and Scottish folk tunes they heard from their masters and adapted the tunes they heard to their instruments. "These strains are no longer known to us," Nathan states, "but it is most likely that many of them were those of the frontier: namely, the folk dance tunes of the British Isles." What this suggests is that the merging of West African and British folk styles, which is the distinguishing mark of American folksong, began to take place during slavery times. Even more significant is the fact that the banjo was one of the main elements in this hybridization. And if, as I have argued, it was the black slaves rather than the white minstrels who developed, albeit from earlier sources, the five-string banjo, then we have another crucial example of the influence of black folk art on our musical culture.

Because it was increasingly removed from the folk community in which it developed, the music of the minstrel banjoists soon lost the flavor of authentic folksong and became a vehicle for the virtuoso instrumentalist. In fact, by the time the vogue of minstrelsy had run its course the banjo ceased to be a Negro instrument—at least in circumstances where its use was likely to be observed by white audiences. This is curious since for almost two hundred years the banjo had been identified as a distinctly Negro instrument. (American genre painters such as George Caleb Bingham and even such sophisticated painters as Henry Tanner and Thomas Eakins painted portraits of blacks playing the five-string banjo.) But partly because of its association with the Negro stereotype propagated by the white minstrels (a view based on the assumption that the slave was a happy-go-lucky, watermelon-eating banjo picker), the five-string banjo became essentially a white man's instrument. (An exception was the use of the five-string banjo by early New Orleans musicians.) It is significant that, although many black folk musicians have attained popularity, none has been strongly associated with the banjo—despite the fact that many can play the instrument. As instrumentalists they have preferred the guitar and I think that this is intimately though not always consciously related to the fact that the banjo smacks too strongly of apologies for slavery, as the following doggerel, advertising a "Southern Version of Uncle Tom's Cabin," performed by a minstrel troupe in 1861, indicates:

> Oh! White Folks, we'll have you to know,
> Dis am not de version of Mrs. Stowe;
> Wid her de Darks am all unlucky,
> But we am de boys of Old Kentucky.
>
> Den hand de Banjo down to play,
> We'll make it ring both night and day;
> And we care not what de white folks say,
> Dey can't get us to run away.[10]

As Alan Lomax pointed out, the banjo became the characteristic instrument of the Southern mountaineer. The manner of transmission is not clear though there have been small numbers of blacks in the mountain areas from early times. Professor Archie Green has suggested to me that the penetration of the mountain areas by railroads using mainly black labor was a major source of contact. However that may be, it is from the playing of Southern Appalachian white banjoists that we have learned most about the style of the instrument. And since that style is not clearly related to the minstrel tradition, it may represent a closer approximation to earlier black styles. Here again the question of tunings is revealing. The minstrels generally tuned their banjos in the following way. (The notes represent the open strings, which actually sound an octave lower.)

As the printed music suggests, this arrangement of notes makes it necessary to finger chords (by pressing the appropriate frets and leaving consonant strings open) to play in a variety of keys without retuning the instrument. But this is not at all like the traditional tunings employed by the mountain banjo pickers.

Buell Kazee, who is not only one of the best Kentucky mountain banjo players but a trained and articulate musician as well, provided me with a dozen tunings that he uses.[11] Most of these are well known to other traditional banjo players, although a few seem to be uniquely related to his own style. As Kazee put it: "The idea of tuning a banjo is to get as many open strings as possible." Thus the basic tunings are an attempt to achieve the triad of the desired tonic chord on the open strings. Although chords are often fretted in addition (ordinarily the subdominant and dominant) the mountain banjo derives its unique sound from the practice of playing the melody on top of the open chord, often with a racing, double time rhythm. And as Kazee pointed out, each tuning has songs that are traditionally associated with it. Here is his tuning for the key of G-major.

A major consequence of this approach is the necessity to retune the banjo in order to play in a different key. (The minstrel players accomplished this by changing the fingering, which is also the practice for most guitarists. But traditional blues guitarists habitually use open tunings— especially in "bottleneck" styles—and it suggests to me that the first blues were probably played on banjo.) Every traditional banjo player will spend a good deal of his time tuning and retuning, which has resulted in a widely-known joke. The banjo picker is asked how long he has been playing. "I've been playing for sixty years," he answers, "and tuning for fifty." The gag turns out to have been a standard one for lutenists in the seventeenth and eighteenth centuries.

For many tunes which might be described as minor in tonality, Kazee takes the G tuning and instead of lowering the third degree a half step (to b-flat) he raises it to c.

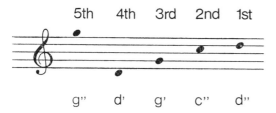

The effects achieved with this tuning, often called "modal," are startling. In fact it is related to an early Church mode (Mixolydian), but the chord produced results in what might better be called a suspended chord, not unlike the tonality of much contemporary music. It is precisely this aspect of folk tradition which Bela Bartok became interested in as a consequence of his collecting trips in Hungary and Romania. In the United States, little attention has been paid to folk instrumental styles by academics, but highly competent studies have been done recently by performers and aficionados.[12]

In its own way, the banjo has been a kind of phoenix of American folk tradition. Unlike the traditional instruments of most European countries, which have fallen into disuse, the banjo has been periodically revived and it is no exaggeration to say that more people play the instrument (often in traditional styles) than ever before. A current instance of the revitalization is the development of "Scruggs style" banjo playing in the context of bluegrass music. The name derives from an instrumentalist, Earl Scruggs, who developed a unique approach to the banjo. With mandolin player Bill Monroe, Scruggs was in a group called the Blue Grass Boys and from around 1945 developed what may be described as a string band in which the banjo was a major solo instrument. (Scruggs provided the background music for the film *Bonnie and Clyde;* although the racing, syncopated banjo seemed perfect for the setting, the irony is that bluegrass music did not actually exist during the time which the film portrays.) Mayne Smith has defined bluegrass as "a style of concert hillbilly music performed by a highly integrated ensemble of voices and nonelectrified stringed instruments, including a banjo played Scruggs-style."[13] It is essentially a white, country music built on the string bands which existed in the twenties and thirties, but Smith points out that "bluegrass clearly shows stylistic links with Northern popular music and jazz. The marked rhythmic stress of the up-beat, the use of improvised solos whereby single musicians dominate the total sound, and the general pattern of ensemble integration are at base African musical practices; but they have reached bluegrass through jazz, at least partially with the mediation of western swing, a hillbilly style that was flourishing in the early 1940's when bluegrass was being developed." Although bluegrass is at the moment not commercially popular, Scruggs' adaptations of traditional picking styles have influenced many musicians, including folk rock and rock instrumentalists. Whatever the future of bluegrass itself, the banjo style associated with it has already assured itself a permanent place in our music.

There are many questions about the history of the banjo that remain unanswered, including the technical issues of manufacture and production. But it seems clear that Alan Lomax was correct in his assertion that the banjo is the locus of a uniquely American folk tradition, based originally on black sources and syncretized with many others thereafter.

Notes

CHAPTER ONE

1. G. S. Kirk has pointed out that the court singer in *The Odyssey* lives in the Phaeacians' town though he is often called upon to sing in the palace. His name "means something like 'pleasing to, or accepted by, the *demos*. . . .' " Kirk concludes that the epic singer "must have sung for popular audiences in houses, taverns or market-place, as well as on special occasions in noble mansions or palaces and at large festivals"; in *The Songs of Homer* (Cambridge, England, 1962), pp. 278–279. Eric A. Havelock has argued that the Homeric poems were a central apparatus for the propagation of social and cultural values and that Plato opposed them on that account; in *Preface to Plato* (Oxford, 1963). The American folk term, "hootenanny," before it was vulgarized by advertising and the mass media, referred to a similar gathering of singers to exhibit their craft and the traditional values contained therein.

2. *The Ballad Revival* (Chicago, 1961), p. 185. Professor Freidman provides a perceptive and balanced estimate of Percy's achievements in chapter seven.

3. Sigrid Bernhard Hustvedt, *Ballad Books and Ballad Men* (Cambridge, Massachusetts, 1930), p. 23.

4. Robert Reinhold Ergang, *Herder and the Foundations of German Nationalism* (New York, 1931), p. 13.

5. *Herder, His Life and Thought* (Berkeley, 1955), p. 249.

6. Herder, in Ergang, pp. 200–201. The original source, as cited by Ergang, is given by the volume and page number of the Suphan Edition of Herder's works, in this case, v, 189–190.

7. Ibid., p. 159; i, 162; ii, 46; i, 165; ii, 49.

8. Ibid., p. 204; ix, 528–529.

9. *Outlines of a Philosophy of the History of Man,* trans. T. Churchill, second ed. (London, 1803), i, 293. Herder's work was originally published in four parts between 1784 and 1791. This is still the only translation available in English. Emerson was familiar with both editions of Churchill's translation.

10. Ibid., i, 388.

11. Ergang, p. 205; i, 18.

12. Clark, p. 259; xxv, 323.

13. Ibid., p. 431.

14. Ibid., p. 260.

15. Isaiah Berlin, "J. G. Herder," *Encounter,* xxv (July 1965), 47. This is part one of two essays, the second of which appears in the August issue of the magazine.

16. F. M. Barnard, *Herder's Social and Political Thought* (London, 1965), pp. 70–71. The following comment from Friedman's brief discussion of Herder typifies the continuing and often subtle attribution to Herder of racist ideas: "A race could not fulfil itself or carry out its sacred duty so long as its unique spirit was contaminated. The *Volkslied* was, thus, one of several touchstones by which the community could measure its approach to, or declension from, purity." *The Ballad Revival,* p. 249.

17. "J. G. Herder," *Encounter,* 38.

18. Ibid., 43.

19. Claude Lévi-Strauss provides evidence to document this point of view in *The Savage Mind* (Chicago, 1966).

20. "The Shaping of the American Character," in Roy Harvey Pearce, ed. *Whitman, A Collection of Critical Essays* (Englewood Cliffs, New Jersey, 1962), p. 145.

CHAPTER TWO

1. *German Culture in America, 1600–1900* (Madison, 1957), p. 110. René Wellek discusses the influence of Herder on Transcendentalist theology in "Emerson and German Philosophy," *The New England Quarterly,* xvi (March 1943), 61. Excerpts from two of Ripley's articles on Herder are reprinted in Perry Miller, ed. *The Transcendentalists* (Cambridge, Massachusetts, 1952), pp. 89, 94.

2. Quoted in Clark, *Herder,* p. 294.

3. Kenneth W. Cameron, *Ralph Waldo Emerson's Reading* (Raleigh, 1941), p. 47. In 1831 Emerson withdrew the two-volume second edition (1803) from the Boston Atheneum.

4. *Freedom and Fate* (Philadelphia, 1953), p. 31.

5. *The Transcendentalists,* p. 8.

6. "From Poe to Valéry," *The Hudson Review,* ii (Autumn, 1949); reprinted in *To Criticize the Critic* (New York, 1965), pp. 27–42.

7. Theodore Spencer, ed. (New York, 1944).

8. Ibid., pp. 211, 213.

9. *American Renaissance* (New York, 1941), p. 58n. Matthiessen does not give the source, but one of my students, Mrs. Elsa Pheeley,

located the passage in Emerson's essay, "Education." Professor William H. Gilman informed me that the passage appears in Emerson's Journal D, now available in Harrison Hayford and A. W. Plumstead, eds. *The Journals and Miscellaneous Notebooks of Ralph Waldo Emerson* (Cambridge, Massachusetts, 1969), VII, 29.

10. Richard Chase traces the "direct influence of Whitman" upon Joyce's *Finnegans Wake,* which he calls "the culminating work, the summa of the contemporary mythic movement in literature. . ."; in *Walt Whitman Reconsidered* (London, 1955), p. 89. I am suggesting that a source of this approach in Whitman is Emerson's esthetic.

11. *The Reign of Wonder* (London, 1965), p. 37.

12. *American Renaissance,* p. 62.

CHAPTER THREE

1. *German Thought in America,* p. 784n.

2. Leslie Fiedler, for example, criticizes Whitman's "Bardic Americanism," maintaining that Whitman fails as a poet when he speaks either as an "American chauvinist" or as a "Romantic internationalist"; in *No! In Thunder* (Boston, 1960), pp. 65, 66. Hans Kohn traced the stream of "extravagant and obsessive nationalism" in Whitman's thought to Herder's "gospel of cultural nationalism." Many critics have agreed with Kohn's assertion that Whitman often sacrificed his poetic genius to "nationalist mysticism"; in *American Nationalism* (New York, 1957), p. 75 ff.

3. Horace I. Traubel, et al., eds. *The Complete Writings of Walt Whitman,* 10 vols. (New York, 1902), III, 66.

4. Cleaveland Rodgers and John Black, eds. *The Gathering of the Forces* (New York, 1920), pp. 238–239.

5. Perry Miller, *The Transcendentalists,* p. 423.

6. "Walt Whitman and his Poems," in Carolyn Wells and Alfred Goldsmith, eds. *Rivulets of Prose* (New York, 1928), p. 9.

7. "Robert Henri and the Emerson-Whitman Tradition," *Publications of the Modern Language Association,* LXXXI (September 1956), 633.

8. *The Complete Poetry and Prose of Walt Whitman* (New York, 1948), I, 26.

9. Ibid., II, 303–304.

10. *Walt Whitman Reconsidered,* p. 92.

11. *American Renaissance,* p. 521.

12. *Symbolism and American Literature* (Chicago, 1953), p. 25.

13. *Studies in Classic American Literature* (New York, 1953), pp. 183–184. (Anchor Books reprint.)

14. The most effective analysis is in the two volume study by Roger Asselineau, *The Evolution of Walt Whitman* (Cambridge, Massachusetts, 1962).

15. Ibid., II, 222.

16. "Style," in A. L. Kroeber, ed. *Anthropology Today* (Chicago, 1953), p. 287.

CHAPTER FOUR

1. "The Poetry of Barbarism," in *Interpretations of Poetry and Religion* (New York, 1957), pp. 176–177. (Harper Torchbook.)

2. "Paleface and Redskin," in *Image and Idea* (New York, 1949), p. 1.

3. The only extended criticism is in Stanley Edgar Hyman, *The Armed Vision* (New York, 1948), chapter five. Brief appreciations of Miss Rourke's pioneering efforts appear in F. O. Matthiessen's *American Renaissance,* Richard Chase's *The American Novel and Its Tradition,* Henry Nash Smith's *Virgin Land,* as well as in numerous works devoted more directly to American folklore or closely related studies.

4. *The Roots of American Culture,* p. 45.

5. Ibid., p. 46.

6. *Trumpets of Jubilee* (New York, 1927).

7. *American Humor,* p. 10. Henceforth, references to this work, in the Anchor Edition, appear in parentheses following the quotation.

8. A definitive study is in Hans Nathan, *Dan Emmett and the Rise of Early Negro Minstrelsy* (Norman, Oklahoma, 1962).

9. *The Armed Vision,* p. 128.

10. *The Roots of American Culture,* pp. 24–25.

11. B. S. Alford, *The Arkansas Traveler* (Little Rock, 1876). Alford's account is quoted in B. A. Botkin, ed. *The Pocket Treasury of American Folklore* (New York, 1950), p. 203.

12. *The Frontier in American History* (New York, 1962), p. 4. This is a reprint of the collection of essays first published in 1920.

13. Blair discusses this technique in the introduction to his *Native American Humor, 1800–1900* (New York, 1937).

14. *Arkansas, A Guide to the State* (New York, 1941), p. 120.

15. *The Writings of Mark Twain* (New York, 1907–1918), XXII, 10–11.

16. It appeared in 1852 and is reprinted in Franklin J. Meine, ed. *Tall Tales of the Southwest* (New York, 1930).

17. *Mark Twain, The Development of a Writer* (Cambridge, Massachusetts, 1962).

CHAPTER FIVE

1. Frederick Louis Ritter, *Music In America* In *America's Music* (New York, 1955), p. xvi.

2. *Native American Ballads* (Philadelphia, 1950), p. 4. For a discussion of the equivocal nature of the term ballad itself, see Louise Pound, *Poetic Origins and the Ballad* (New York, 1921), p. 39 ff.

3. *The Traditional Tunes of the Child Ballads* (Princeton, 1959), p. xii.

4. Ibid., p. xvii.

5. Helen Child Sargent and George Lyman Kitteredge, eds. *English and Scottish Popular Ballads* (Boston, 1904), p. xii.

6. Ibid., p. xiii. Louise Pound points out that in 1915 Kittredge commented "that if he were summing up the facts he would modify his statement that ballad-singing is a lost art, either in Great Britain or the United States . . . but the statement that ballad-making is a lost art he did not modify"; *Poetic Origins and the Ballad,* p. 231n.

7. *Anglo-American Folksong Scholarship* (New Brunswick, New Jersey, 1959).

8. *Ballad Books and Ballad Men,* p. 238.

9. Stanley Edgar Hyman, "The Child Ballad in America," *Journal of American Folklore,* LXX (1957), 239.

10. "On the Field and Work of a Journal of American Folk-Lore," *Journal of American Folklore,* I (1888), 4.

11. *Journal of American Folklore,* XXVIII (January–March 1915), 3.

12. *English Folk Songs from the Southern Appalachians* (London, 1917), pp. xxxvi–xxxvii.

13. "New World Analogues of the English and Scottish Popular Ballads," *Mid-West Quarterly,* III (April, 1916), 176. The existence of Negro materials among the cowboy songs illustrates the fact that there were large numbers of Negro cowboys on the range, though their presence was not acknowledged by most historians. A correction of this oversight is in Philip Durham and Everett L. Jones, *The Negro Cowboys* (New York, 1965).

14. *White and Negro Spirituals* (New York, 1943), p. 285. It is worth noting that Jackson is one of the major proponents of the idea that Negro spirituals are completely derivative of white traditions.

15. James Weldon Johnson, *God's Trombones* (New York, 1927), p. 3.

16. For a full discussion of this view, see Melville J. Herskovits, *The Myth of the Negro Past* (New York, 1941), reprinted as a Beacon paperback.

17. In an early article John Lomax noted that the Negro's song tradition is "so unique, so pliable, that no other folk music in America approaches it in perfection." But at that time he identified the dominant theme in Negro songs as "self-pity"; "Self-Pity in Negro Folk-Songs," *The Nation,* cv (August 9, 1917), 141–145. Lomax's shift in attitude may show the increasing influence of Alan Lomax's point of view. Despite the close collaboration of father and son in the later works, John Lomax apparently retained elements of the white Southerner's attitude toward the Negro. Pete Seeger has described to me a newsreel film in which John Lomax is exceedingly condescending and patronizing toward Leadbelly. Charles Seeger recalls an incident during the time that Leadbelly was working as John Lomax's chauffeur in the course of a collecting trip in the South. Leadbelly demanded a salary and Lomax was infuriated. Seeger notes that Lomax thought of Leadbelly as a member of the family who would be given money when he needed it rather than on a salary basis. Alan Lomax recalls that the problems between his father and Leadbelly stemmed in part from the conflict of two strong-willed men. However this may be, there is no doubt that John Lomax and his son agreed in their final estimates of the meaning of Negro song traditions.

18. Carl Engel, "Views and Reviews," *Musical Quarterly,* xxi (1935), 108; quoted in D. K. Wilgus, *Anglo-American Folksong Scholarship,* p. 217.

19. Alan Lomax has continued his concern with the issues I have discussed in, *Folk Song Style and Culture* (Washington, D.C., 1968). With a group of co-workers, Lomax has tried to chart world folksong styles in order to show that "no branch of the human family, no matter how well- or ill-equipped technically, fails to symbolize its social norms in a suitable song style. Each culture raises its voice in a way that speaks for its economy, its sexual mores, its degree of stratification, its ways of organizing groups, etc."

EPILOGUE

1. *The New Golden Bough* (New York, 1959), pp. xviii–xix. (Mentor Edition.)

2. (Cambridge, Massachusetts, 1933), p. 5.

3. Eliot's essay, which is now widely reprinted, appeared originally in the collection, *The Sacred Wood* (1920).

4. Seeger's comments are from "Woody Guthrie, Songwriter," *Ramparts,* November 30, 1968, pp. 28–33.

5. Compare Dylan's first album, entitled "Bob Dylan," with later ones that show the shift from Guthrie's style—notably, "The Times They Are A-Changin' " and especially "Blonde on Blonde." (These are all Columbia recordings.)

6. (New York, 1968), p. 80.

7. Ibid., p. 81.

APPENDIX

1. Ed. Eric Blom (London, 1954), I, 402.

2. Ibid., 403.

3. Adrienne Koch and William Pcdcn, eds. *The Life and Selected Writings of Thomas Jefferson* (New York, 1944), p. 258n.

4. *America's Music*, p. 67.

5. Frederick Grunfeld, *The Art and Times of the Guitar* (London, 1969), pp. 148, 151.

6. "Joel Walker Sweeney and the First Banjo," *Los Angeles County Museum Quarterly,* VII (Spring, 1949), 7–11.

7. *The History of Musical Instruments* (New York, 1940), p. 134.

8. I, 402.

9. "Early Banjo Tunes and American Syncopation," *The Musical Quarterly,* XLII (October, 1956), 466.

10. From a poster in the Theater Collection of the Houghton Library, Harvard University.

11. Gene Bluestein, ed. "Buell Kazee Sings and Plays," Folkways Recording, FS 3810, 12″ lp.

12. See Pete Seeger, *How To Play the Five-String Banjo*, revised edition (Oak Publications, New York); and John Burke, *Old Time Fiddle Tunes for Banjo* (Amsco Music Publications, New York).

13. "An Introduction to Bluegrass," *Journal of American Folklore,* LXXVII (July–September, 1965), p. 246.

Index